C000205585

CAMMELL LAIRD BUILT WARSHIPS

by Alistair Lofthouse

The battleship ***HMS Prince of Wales*** seen as she is moored in Cammell Laird's wet basin on the day of her launch on 3 May 1939. One of five King George V class battleships, which was the last major class of battleship built for the Royal Navy, she would be lost with the lives of 327 crew just over two years later.

ACKNOWLEDGEMENTS

With thanks to the staff of Wirral Archives Service, who looked after much of the material from Cammell Laird up to 1993.
archives@wirral.gov.uk

This book would not have been possible without the kind support of BAE Systems.

Also thanks to Cammell Laird Shiprepairers & Shipbuilders Limited for providing pictures of their work on the Queen Elizabeth class aircraft carriers.
www.cammell-laird.com

First published in the United Kingdom in 2016 by NavyBooks, Unit 6B, Heathlands Business Park, Liskeard, Cornwall, PL14 4DH

Cammell Laird Built Warships

In 1810 William Laird first arrived in Liverpool. Although later the 30 year old Scotsman would found one of the most famous ship building companies, this was not the reason why he was in Liverpool. His father owned a ropeworks in Greenock and he was hoping to gain orders from shipping companies in the area. In this he was not succesful but he was an energetic businessman.

He soon became a director of two shipping companies plus, more importantly, he became an agent for Watt's Steam Engines. William also thought that there was great potential for new docks at Birkenhead across the Mersey from the bustling Liverpool Docks so he started to buy land in the Birkenhead area. He also had plans to construct a canal from Birkenhead to the River Dee that would allow a safer route for shipping avoiding the shifting mud banks of the Mersey.

For these plans he would need investment, and a lot of it, which would take time. In the meantime he used his land purchased north of the Wallasey Pool to base his boiler works, building Watt's boilers. This company, founded in 1824, was named the Birkenhead Iron Works.

The investment for the docks never came but in 1828 William's son John, a solicitor by profession, joined the company. It occurred to John that in producing boilers for ships they had the skills and the site for producing complete ships. A year later they delivered their first ship, ***Wye***, built for Irish Inland Steam which was followed by two more.

In 1830 they produced a paddle steamer for the same company which was fitted with watertight bulkheads, a feature years before its time. The Lairds considered that iron ships were the future, much against the beliefs of the British Admiralty and London Ship insurance companies. The disadvantages of wood were not only the dwindling supply in Britain but also the fitting of modern steam boilers put tremendous strains structurally on wooden ships. It also required the use of short lengths of wood which would therefore have many joints and weak points.

Such was their belief that they commissioned the Astronomer Royal, Professor Airey, to show that although the iron used in their ships affected compass readings this could be compensated for by what is known now as deviation. The company struggled in the late 1830s but by the 1840s the Admiralty had decided that iron ships were the future and ordered five frigates from the Lairds. The first ***HMS Birkenhead*** became a troopship famously sinking off the Cape of Good Hope after striking a submerged rock.

Lairds had done so well they managed to build fine quality buildings for their workers and built the famous Hamilton Square in Birkenhead. Today their legacy is not only a very high percentage of listed buildings in the area but also a public park donated to the town by the Lairds.

In 1863, despite much opposition, Lairds built the Confederate commercial raider ***Alabama***, interestingly built out of wood. Attempts were made to stop her delivery to the Confederates but she simply did not return after her sea trials and was transferred to her crew off the Azores.

John Laird retired from the business in 1861 becoming, two years later, the first Member of Parliament for Birkenhead, the business passing to his sons William, John and Henry.

By 1900 the site used by Lairds was too small and expansion was needed so that they could build the larger ships now being required. Merging with John Jones & Sons to form the Tranmere Bay Development Company they increased the yard to 98.5 acres including the 15 acre wet fitting-out basin which was the largest private wet dock in Britain. Six new slipways were built, the biggest able to take a 1,000 feet long ship. Two new dry docks were built and also a complete internal railway system.

In 1903 with the backing of the Admiralty the company, then known as Laird Bros & Company Ltd, merged with the large Sheffield steel producing company of Charles Cammell & Company Ltd, the intention being that this new vast company would have access to all the processes needed to build ships from start to finish. Charles Cammell had the Cyclops and Grimesthorpe steelworks in Sheffield, ordnance works in Coventry, coalmines, iron ore mines and smelting works at Worthington. The new business became known as Cammell Laird & Co Ltd.

The early 20th Century were slow years and the last of the Lairds left the firm. However, in 1909 work started to pick up with the Admiralty placing many orders, including the battleship ***Audacious*** and what was then the largest floating dock in the world, able to lift a ship of 32,000 tons.

WW1 resulted in busy years for Cammell Laird but the company's great achievement was designing new boilers for the Admiralty resolving the problem of boiler explosions that were occurring due to the high demands of WW1 naval warfare. Some 50 warships were fitted with these new boilers before the end of the war.

The end of World War I brought a reduction of work. Cammell Laird managed to continue but during the great depression in 1931 only one ship was on the order book. The tide changed in 1935 with the order for the third ***Ark Royal***. She was only the second warship to be designed from the beginning as an aircraft carrier and was, at the time, the biggest ship to be launched into the Mersey. There then followed a build up of orders leading up to WWII. During the six years of the war 106 warships were built, almost one every 20 days. They were so busy that ships were often launched by the management.

Post war the yard had to change to largely commercial work as naval orders diminished. The fourth ***Ark Royal***, however, kept the yard busy until 1955. She became the Royal Navy's largest warship until the advent of the Queen Elizabeth Class aircraft carriers in the 2010s for which Cammell Laird built a number of the flight deck blocks.

The early 1960's saw modernisation of the yard including a new dry dock, 'Princess Dock', which was 950 feet long and could accommodate the largest ships built or planned. Naval orders included the first guided missile destroyer ***Devonshire*** and in 1963 two nuclear powered Polaris submarines were ordered that increased the workforce by 40% giving a total of just over 11,000 in 1969. By this time Cammell Laird were losing commercial work to companies in the East which in 1970 resulted in the government buying half the company. The Sheffield operations had been absorbed into British Steel during the 1960s and today is part of Sheffield Forgemasters.

Full nationalisation occurred in 1977 but in 1985 the yard was denationalised and became a subsidiary of Vickers Shipbuilding which built three of the four Upholder submarines. Originally a class of 12 boats was planned but the end of the Cold War saw no further orders. With no commercial work Cammell Laird closed in 1993.

Within two years new owners re-opened the yard for ship repairs using around one third of the original site. After various owners the yard was taken over by Northwest Ship repairers in 2006 which had MoD contracts to maintain 11 Royal Fleet Auxiliary ships for some 25 years. In 2010 they commenced working on flight deck blocks for ***Queen Elizabeth*** and ***Prince of Wales***.

Alistair Lofthouse
2016

Cammell Laird in 1951. ***HMS Ark Royal*** *is fitting out in the wet basin which would take a further four years to complete. All other work appears to be commercial.*

HCS Nemesis (YN: 0028) was launched in 1839 and was the first British ocean-going iron warship. Commissioned for the East India Company in 1840, she had watertight bulkheads, the first time they had been used in a warship. She was the first iron ship to sail around the Cape of Good Hope and had a shallow draft which enabled her to travel into rivers. During the first Opium Wars she sank the ***Cambridge***, an American merchantman, that the Chinese had purchased. ***HCS Nemesis*** accompanied the British fleet up river and due to her shallow draught was able to move through shallow waters to aid the capture of Canton. Later, she was tasked with the suppression of pirates in Indonesia and the Philippines and was last seen in the 1850s in Burmese waters.

One of the first iron-hulled ships built for the Royal Navy, and initially named ***HMS Vulcan***, the steam frigate ***HMS Birkenhead*** (YN: 0051) was renamed in 1845 in honour of her birthplace. Before commissioning she was reclassified as a troopship and the intended armament of two 96-pdr pivot guns was not fitted. She was a steam paddle ship with sails, displaced 1,916 tons, and was designed by John Laird. Whilst she was under construction, technology was moving on and the Royal Navy adopted propeller propulsion that led to ***HMS Birkenhead*** being converted for the transportation of troops around the British Empire. Her career though was short. She was lost on 26 February 1852 off the Weston Cape, South Africa, whilst carrying troops and their families, after hitting an uncharted rock at night. Only 193 out of 640 onboard survived. The ordering of the men to stay on board, letting women and children leave first, is believed to be the first such case of this practice. Today there is a memorial to the sinking near the Birkenhead ferry terminal.

CSS Alabama (YN: 0290) was a screw sloop-of-war built in secret for the Confederate States Navy being completed in 1862. Launched as ***Enrica*** on 15 May 1862 she was a mix of sail and steam armed with British made guns. She had two successful years serving as a commercial raider attacking Union merchant and naval vessels. She never docked in a Southern port. Her end came on 11 June 1864 at the Battle of Cherbourg when the Union warship ***USS Kearsarge*** sank her after the ***Alabama*** had fired 370 rounds at the ***Kearsarge***. 41 of her 150 crew died in the action.

HMS Agincourt (YN: 0291) was a Minotaur class armoured frigate. She was laid down on 30 October 1861 and launched on 27 March 1865. Owing to many changes to her design she was not completed until 1868. In 1871 she was nearly lost when she grounded on Pearl Rock near Gibraltar. During the Russo-Turkish War of 1877-78 ***HMS Agincourt*** was sent as part of a force to deter any Russian advance on Constantinople. She spent most of her career as the flagship of the Channel Fleet's second-in-command. She was present for Queen Victoria's Jubilee Fleet Review in 1897 and was subsequently used at Portland as a Training ship. Renamed ***Boscawen III*** in 1904, she was moved to Harwich in 1905 and became ***Ganges II*** where she stayed until 1909 before moving to Sheerness to become a coal hulk for the next 50 years. She was finally scrapped in 1960.

Secretly ordered by the Confederate States of America in 1862 under the cover of being the Egyptian warship ***El Tousson, HMS Scorpion*** (YN: 0294) was originally intended to be ***CSS North Carolina***. However, in 1863 the British Government seized the vessel, together with her sister (***HMS Wivern***) then being built by Laird. She was an ironclad turret ship armed with four 9-inch muzzle loading guns mounted in two turrets, barque rigged with Laird built steam powered twin screw propulsion. Commissioning in the Royal Navy in 1865 ***Scorpion*** served the Channel Fleet until 1869. Her rig was reduced from a barque to a schooner when she transferred to Bermuda to act as a harbour and coastal defence ship. After 30 years service she was sunk as a target in 1901. She was raised a year later and sold in 1903 to be scrapped in the USA, however, she sank whilst on transit.

Built for the Confederate Navy under the cover of an Egyptian warship ***El Monassir*** was laid down in April 1862. A couple of months after her launch in October 1863 she was seized by the British government and completed in 1865 as ***HMS Wivern*** (YN: 0295). Her career started in the British Channel Fleet with a period from 1868 as a coastal defence ship based in the Humber. After a time in reserve at Hull she was sent to Hong Kong in 1886, serving there during the Boxer Rebellion of 1900. Reduced to harbour duties from 1904 she was sold for scrap in 1922. She had been noted for her poor sea handling qualities - in heavy seas she would roll 27 degrees. In this image the two turrets mounting twin 9-inch muzzle loading guns can be seen.

An ironclad turret ship built for the Peruvian Navy, she was designed by Captain Cowper Phipps Coles who designed ***HMS Captain***. ***Huascar*** (YN: 0321) was built in 1865 and she is preserved today near the naval dockyard in Talcahuano, Chile. She is of the same vintage as ***HMS Warrior*** preserved at Portsmouth. She first served in a Peruvian-Chilean squadron that was sent to Callao to fight the Spanish but arrived too late and the revolution was over. Captured in 1877 by rebels in the Peruvian civil war, her attacks on British merchant ships brought her into conflict with the Royal Navy ships ***Shah*** and ***Amethyst*** in the inconclusive Battle of Pacocha in May 1877. During the War of the Pacific (1879-83) she was captured by Chile after a battle in which 64 of her 193 crew were killed. She was decommissioned in 1901 becoming a tender. Since 1952 she has been a museum ship and is open to the public.

Ordered by the Royal Netherlands Navy as an enlarged version of the Scorpion class ironclad turret ships originally ordered by the Confederate States, ***HNLMS Prins Hendrik der Nederlanden*** (YN: 0330) was laid down in 1865, launched the following October and commissioned in March 1867. She was built with a strengthened bow for using as a ram against other ships. Most of her service was in the Dutch East Indies becoming an ammunition hulk in 1899. She was scrapped in 1925. The above photographs are some of the earliest taken at Lairds.

An unsuccessful design, carried out by Captain Cowper Phipps Coles, much against the wishes of the Admiralty. ***HMS Captain*** (YN: 0346) was a masted turret ship laid down on 30 January 1867 and launched on 27 March 1869. During her construction Coles had been ill and was unable to supervise the work at Laird's. On her commissioning in April 1870 it was discovered that the ship was some 735 tons heavier than planned. Early trials were successful but five months after completion, whilst she sailed off Cape Finisterre on 6 September 1870 in a force six wind, she began to heel over. Most navy ships of the time could roll 60 degrees but due to ***Captain's*** low freeboard she could only roll 21 degrees. Despite attempts to cut the sails she capsized taking with her 480 men with just 18 saved. An inquiry concluded that the ship was unstable. The report reads: "*the **Captain** was built in deference to public opinion expressed in Parliament and through other channels, and in opposition to views and opinions of the Controller and his Department*".

The steam corvette ***ARA Uruguay*** (YN: 0409) was ordered in 1872 as part of Argentina's modernisation programme. She was launched on 6 March 1874, commissioning in July that year, displacing 550 tons with a length of 152 feet. Initially, she was employed as a gunboat armed with four Vavasseur mounted 7-inch guns, one mounted forward, one astern and the other two port and starboard. In 1890 the armament was changed to two 90mm and one 150mm Armstrong guns and later in 1893 changed to two 120mm and two 66mm Armstrong guns. In 1878 she took part in an expedition south of Santa Cruz River, along with the monitor ***Los Andes*** and the gunboat ***Constitucion***, to assert Argentina's claim of sovereignty to Patagonia, which Chile also claimed. In 1884 she embarked a scientific party to observe the Transit of Venus and in 1903 she was converted into a rescue ship intended for service in the Antarctic. De-commissioned in 1926 to become an ammunition hulk she was rebuilt as a museum ship in 1954. She is preserved today in Buenos Aires near another preserved Laird built ship, the training vessel ***Presidente Sarmiento*** that dates from 1897.

(Image courtesy of Bob Flanagan)

HMS Rattlesnake (YN: 0537) was a unique design of Torpedo Gunboat of the Royal Navy. Laid down in November 1885, launched in 1886 she was commissioned in May 1887. It was intended that the ship should hunt smaller torpedo boats but her design became obsolete very rapidly as torpedo boat destroyers appeared. She became a target ship in 1906 before being scrapped in 1910.

The Royal Sovereign class battleship ***HMS Royal Oak*** (YN: 0579), was launched on 5 November 1892. She arrived at Portsmouth 11 months later for fitting out and she was commissioned in June 1894. At 14,150 tons, with main armament of four 13.5-inch guns, the Royal Sovereign class were considered the best all round battleships of their era. ***HMS Royal Oak*** served in Home and Mediterranean waters. By 1906 she was outclassed by the new Dreadnought class battleships and spent the next six years in reserve until she was sold for scrap in January 1914.

HMS Contest (YN: 0599), one of the Banshee class of Torpedo Boat Destroyers, was launched on 1 December 1894 and completed in 1895. Displacing 280 tons she was armed with a single 12-pdr gun forward and two bow torpedo tubes. The above photo seems to show her on trials with no armament and no flag. She served in Home waters before being broken up in 1911. Two further members of the class were built by Laird, ***HMS Banshee*** (YN: 0598) launched in November 1984, serving mostly in the Mediterranean and broken up in 1912 and ***HMS Dragon*** (YN: 0600) launched on 15 December 1894, serving in the Mediterranean and scrapped in 1912.

The pre-Dreadnought battleship ***HMS Mars*** (YN: 0603) was a member of the nine strong Majestic class, laid down in 1894 and launched in March 1896, commissioning a year later. Regarded as being the finest class of warship of the day, the Majestics provided the blueprint for British battleship design for the following decade. Displacing 16,000 tons fully loaded her armament comprised four 12-inch, twelve 6-inch guns, sixteen 12-pdr and twelve 3-pdr guns. The class was based on the earlier Royal Sovereign class battleships but had much improved Harvey hardfaced steel armour and a main armament which used cordite instead of black powder. The gun turrets were also fully enclosed.

HMS Mars was present at Queen Victoria's Diamond Jubilee at Spithead in 1897. In 1902 eleven men were killed in the forward gun turret when the guns were fired before the breech was closed. Most of her service was in Home waters. She was based at Dover at the beginning of WW1. By 1915 she was considered obsolete and was disarmed and converted to a troopship, her 12-inch guns and mountings being re-used in the Lord Clive class monitors. Serving in the Dardanelles Campaign she evacuated allied troops from Anzac Cove in December 1915 and was later used as a depot ship. She was finally scrapped in 1921.

One of nineteen Quail class torpedo boat destroyers, ***HMS Sparrowhawk*** (YN: 0607) was laid down on 30 May 1895, launched in October the same year and commissioned in 1897. Fitted with two triple expansion engines for a designed speed of 30 knots in trials, she achieved a speed of 30.2 knots. She was armed with two 18-inch torpedo tubes, one 12-pdr and five 6-pdr guns. She took part in the Naval Review off Spithead on 26 June 1897 to celebrate the Diamond Jubilee of Queen Victoria. Afterwards she was sent to the Pacific station and then to the China station where, in 1904, she struck an uncharted rock off the mouth of theYangtze river. There were no casualties but the ship was lost.

HMS Thrasher (YN: 0608) a Quail class 30 knotter Torpedo Destroyer was laid down in May 1895, launched on 5 November 1895 and commissioned in June 1897. This class of warship had been built due to concern the Admiralty had over new, faster, foreign ships that were entering service. The Quail class were capable of 30 knots, some three knots faster than had been standard before. On 29 September 1897, whilst with the destroyer ***Lynx*** she ran aground in a fog off Dodman Point, Cornwall. The grounding caused a steam main aboard ***Thrasher*** to rupture, killing four stokers. After repairs the ship was never as fast as her sisters. On 8 February 1917 she was sailing off Flamborough Head when she spotted the German submarine ***UC-39*** engaging allied merchants ships on the surface. After being attacked with depth charges as she dived, the damaged submarine surfaced only to be finished off by ***Thrasher's*** guns. After the end of WW1 she was sold for scrap.

The fourth out of 13 Quail class built by Lairds was ***HMS Virago*** (YN: 0609), laid down in June 1895, launched on 19 November 1895 and completed in June 1897. Displacing some 390 tons, with a crew of 58, this was another class of warship from the period when the Admiralty gave a broad specification to the builders with the intention of the builders carrying out the detailed design. Together with her sisters she was present at the Naval Review at Spithead in celebration of the Diamond Jubilee on 26 June 1897. Later, with her sister ***Sparrowhawk***, she served on the Pacific and China stations. In October 1913 all four funnel 30-knot turtleback destroyers were classified as 'B' or Quail class. Although built to the same Admiralty specification they were not a true class as detailed design had varied from builder to builder. She was due to be sold in 1914, but the sale was cancelled due to the outbreak of WW1. She was scrapped in 1919.

HMS Glory (YN: 0630) was a member of the six strong Canopus class pre-Dreadnoughts designed for use in the Far East to counter the rapidly expanding Japanese Navy. Launched in 1899 she was completed in 1900 at a cost of £780,000. Her armament comprised 4 x 12-inch guns and 12 x 6-inch guns. The class was 2,000 tons lighter than the preceding Majestic class and were the first battleships fitted with water-tube boilers, giving greater steam power and increased speed. She served on the China Station until 1905. After refitting in 1907 she served in the Mediterranean Fleet. Her WW1 service included Canada, West Indies, Mediterranean, Dardannelles Campaign and Suez. Finally, she was based at Archangel, being part of the North Russian Squadron. Paying off in 1919, she was renamed ***Crescent*** and reassigned the role of depot ship until she was scrapped in 1922.

The Russian Torpedo boat destroyer ***IRN Som*** (YN: 0637) was completed in 1899. She was based on the then current design of British Torpedo Boat Destroyer which was essentially a Quail class 30 knot destroyer. Cammell Laird were building a number of these at the time for the Royal Navy. Renamed ***Boyevoy*** in March 1902, she was torpedoed by a Japanese picket boat on 27 April 1904 but made it to Port Arthur, Australia, before being scuttled by her crew on 2 January 1905 to prevent her capture by the Japansese.

Duncan class Pre-Dreadnought ***HMS Exmouth*** (YN: 0638) was launched in 1901 to be fitted out, armed and completed for sea at Chatham in 1903, at a cost of £1,098,000. With a top speed of 19 knots she had a range of 7,000 miles. She served in the Mediterranean, Channel and Atlantic fleets prior to WW1 and during the conflict she fought in the Dardanelles campaign as well as service in Home Waters and the Aegean Sea. She ended her war service on the East Indies Station. By January 1918 ***Exmouth*** was being used as an accommodation ship before being sold for scrap in 1920 to the Forth Shipbreaking Co.

A Laird Type River class destroyer ***HMS Foyle*** (YN: 0649), was named after the Irish River. She was laid down in June 1902, launched on 25 February 1903 and is seen above having one of her two Vertical Triple Expansion steam engines lowered into her. The intention had been to mount five 6-pdr guns, as fitted to the earlier Quail class turtleback destroyers, but in 1906 this was changed to three 12-pdr. On commissioning, in 1904, she was based at Harwich. In 1914 she moved to Portsmouth to become part of the Dover Patrol which, from 1917, started providing convoys in the English Channel. On 15 March 1917 ***Foyle*** struck a contact mine laid by German submarine ***UC-68*** off Plymouth with the loss of 28 men and although an attempt was made to salvage her she sank whilst under tow.

Thirty-four River class vessels were ordered from six shipyards of which Lairds built nine. ***HMS Arun*** (YN: 0651) was laid down in August 1902, launched the following April and completed in February 1904. She was sent to the East Coast Destroyer Flotilla of the 1st Fleet and based at Harwich. On 13 August 1904 she collided with the destroyer ***Decoy*** off the Isles of Scilly, causing the latter to sink. She spent most of WW1 in the Mediterranean Fleet based at Alexandria, returning home in 1919. She was sold for scrap to T. W. Ward of Sheffield and was broken up in 1920 at Hale, Cornwall.

Laid down on 27 August 1902, ***HMS Blackwater*** (YN: 0652) was launched on 25 July 1903 and commissioned the following March. Initial service was with the East Coast Destroyer Flotilla of the 1st Fleet and based at Harwich. On 6 April 1909 ***Blackwater*** sank, after a collision with the merchantman ***SS Hero*** off Dungeness, in the English Channel.

The first member of the four-strong Diamond class, 3rd Class Protected Cruisers, ***HMS Topaze*** (YN: 0653) was laid down in August 1902 and commissioned in November 1904. A successor to the Pelorus class they were, at over 3,000 tons and 373 feet long, very much larger than the earlier ships. The Cammell Laird ships were fitted with two triple expansion steam engines driving two shafts. A sister, ***Amethyst,*** built by Armstrong, was different being the first British cruiser to be built with turbine machinery, three steam turbines powering three shafts to evaluate the performance. The turbines proved more economical at high speeds but less so at slower speeds. Cammell Laird also built her sister ship ***Diamond*** (YN: 0654) which was completed in 1905. Both had rather uneventful WW1 service starting in the Channel Fleet then moving in 1915 to the Mediterranean where they took part in the Dardanelles operation. ***HMS Topaze*** then moved to the East Indies in 1917 where she stayed until the end of the war. Both vessels were sold for scrap in 1921.

HMS Pathfinder (YN: 0655) the lead ship of the Pathfinder class of scout cruisers, was laid down in August 1903, launched on 16 July 1904 and commissioned in July 1905. Eight ships of the class were ordered but detailed design was left to the individual shipyards which in effect resulted in four sub-classes. At the outbreak of the WW1, ***Pathfinder*** became the leader of the 8th Destroyer Flotilla operating from the Firth of Forth and was torpedoed by ***U-21*** off St. Abb's Head on 5 September 1914. The torpedo hit forward and detonated the magazine which resulted in the ship breaking in two, sinking within four minutes with the loss of 259 of her crew of 289. The attack was the first ever by a submarine fired torpedo that resulted in the loss of a warship. At the time the Admiralty declared the loss was due to a mine as it was still largely thought that submarines were incapable of sinking a warship.

The second Pathfinder class built by Cammell Lairds, ***HMS Patrol*** (YN: 0658), the only ship to bear this name, was laid down in October 1903. She launched the following October and commissioned in 1915 with a build cost of £280,000. She was based at Hartlepool with her sister ***Forward*** and the destroyers ***Doon***, ***Waveney***, ***Moy*** and ***Test***. On 16 December 1914 the destroyers put to sea without the cruisers and encountered a German Squadron of ships including ***Seydlitz***, ***Moltke*** and the cruiser ***Blücher***. The destroyers chased off the German vessels which went on to shell Hartlepool. ***HMS Patrol*** sailed from Hartlepool but was engaged by ***Blücher***, being hit by two heavy shells. Though the Germans broke off the attack ***Patrol*** ran aground at the entrance to the Tees. She was refloated and limped to Middlesborough Docks. After repairs in 1915 she joined the 7th Destroyer Flotilla in the Humber, decommissioning in 1919 and being scrapped in Holland the following year.

The River, or Erne, class destroyer ***HMS Liffey*** (YN: 0659), was named after the river which flows through Dublin. She was ordered under the 1903-04 Naval Estimates and was completed in May 1905. The design of the class was a new departure for British destroyers as seaworthiness was given higher priority than speed. They proved to be reliable vessels, capable of maintaining high speeds in most sea conditions. ***HMS Liffey*** spent her entire wartime career in home waters, being fitted with depth charges for anti-submarine patrols. In 1919 she was sold to T.W. Ward for breaking up at Grays Essex.

The final River class officially ordered from Cammell Laird by the Admiralty, ***HMS Moy*** (YN: 0660), was laid down in March 1904 and commissioned in June 1905. Her pre-war service was with her sisters at Harwich. Her early WW1 employment was in the Firth of Forth where she carried out anti-submarine patrols. On 16 December 1914 - under the Division Leader ***Doon*** along with ***Waveney***, ***Test*** - ***Moy***, under the command of Lieutenant C. C. Naylor, was sent to patrol off Hartlepool. During the German Battlecruiser raid on Hartlepool, she was damaged by German shellfire. She was struck by fragments from a shell, bursting short and suffered splinter damage. There were no casualties. Two further members of the class ***Ouse*** (YN: 0661) and ***Test*** (YN: 0663) were built speculatively by Cammell Lairds in 1905. They were purchased by the Admiralty in 1909 and both served in WW1. They were sold, with ***Moy***, for scrap in 1919.

HMS Cossack (YN: 0667) was laid down in November 1905. She was the lead member of the five strong Cossack class. In 1904 the First Sea Lord, Jackie Fisher, proposed that the next class of destroyer should make at least 33 knots and should use oil fired boilers and steam turbines. The result was the Tribal class of 15 ships and, as with earlier classes of destroyer, the specification was issued by the Admiralty but the individual builders carried out final design so there was little commonality within the class. She was commissioned in April 1908 and achieved a speed of over 34 knots, however, she rolled heavily and was said to be very wet forward. During WW1 she served in the North Sea and the English Channel with the 6th Destroyer Flotilla. On 1 July 1917, ***Cossack*** collided with the transport ***SS The Duchess*** near Eastbourne. ***Cossack's*** depth charges exploded as a result of the collision, sinking ***The Duchess*** and blowing off ***Cossack's*** stern. ***HMS Cossack*** was towed to Dover for repair and was scrapped in 1919.

At the time the largest destroyer in the Royal Navy, ***HMS Swift*** (YN: 0671) was a unique experimental ship built on the orders of Admiral Fisher, who wanted a force of fast destroyers capable of 36 knots instead of the normal 25. Laid down in 1906 and launched on 7 December 1907, her displacement of 1,825 tons was over twice that of a standard destroyer. With half her length being devoted to machinery, in consequence the ship was lightly armed. Her cost was also twice that of a standard destroyer. During trials, in 1910, she failed to reach her intended speed and after modifications she reached 35 knots, slightly slower than intended. Admiral Fisher's retirement brought an end to such experimental vessels. In April 1917 ***Swift***, alongside ***Broke,*** was involved in the Battle of Dover Strait. In this confusing battle they encountered six German destroyers, two of which, ***G.85*** and ***G.42,*** were sunk and ***Broke*** badly damaged. After being involved with the Zeebrugge raid of 1918 she was paid off and sold for scrap in 1921.

HMS Wolverine (YN: 0692) was a member of the 16 strong Beagle class destroyer, the last such to be built for the Royal Navy with coal fired boilers. Launched in January 1910 she was completed in September of that year. In trials she reached 27 knots. The above picture is probably of ***Wolverine*** on her builder's speed trials. On completion she joined the Home Fleet transferring to the Mediterranean in 1912 seeing action at both the Dardanelles and Gallipoli. Returning to the UK in 1917 to join the 2nd Flotilla based in Northern Ireland, she was lost on 12 December after a collision with the sloop ***Rosemary***. Her sistership ***Renard*** (YN: 0691) completed in September 1910 and was sold for scrap in August 1920.

Laid down as ***San-Luis*** (YN: 0698) for Argentina in 1911, she was a member of the 12 strong Catamarca destroyer class, of which four were built by Cammell Lairds, four in Germany and four in France. Only the four German ships were delivered to Argentina, the four Laird built ships going to Greece in 1912 as the Aetos class. ***San-Luis*** became ***Aetos*** meaning wild beast. She served throughout WW1 and was rebuilt by J. Samuel White on the Isle of Wight. From 1925-27, and after the invasion of Greece, she served with the Royal Navy in the Indian Ocean until finally being scrapped in 1945.

Completed as ***IHN Panthir*** (YN: 0700) for the Greek Navy she had been ordered as the Argentine ***Santiago*** but, together with her three Cammell Laird built sisters, was purchased by Greece in 1912, a year after they had been launched. Although they resembled British destroyers of the time they had American-pattern 4-inch guns supplied by Bethlehem Steel. She was modernised between 1925-27 in the UK by J. Samuel White, together with her sisters ***IHN Aetos***, ***IHN Leon*** (YN: 0699) and ***IHN Lerax*** (YN: 0701). Post modernisation they had two funnel vessels, resembling British 'W' type ships, and their speed was increased by two knots. ***IHN Leon*** was sunk on 22 April 1941 by German forces. Her sisters were scrapped post war.

The Acheron class of 23 destroyers was redesignated the 'I' class in 1913. Fourteen were built as Admiralty 'I' class to a standard design, with the remaining nine ships being builder specials resulting in significant differences across the class. ***HMS Lizard*** (YN: 0714), named after the Lizard peninsula in the county of Cornwall, was laid down on 1 January 1911 and launched that October. She served in the battles of Heligoland Bight and Jutland. In January 1918 she was involved in the Battle of Imbros where German-Turkish ships ***Breslau*** and ***Goeben*** engaged ***Lizard***, ***Tigress***, and the monitors ***Raglan*** and ***M28***. The British were outclassed, losing ***M28*** and ***Tigress***, however, both ***Beslau*** and ***Goeben*** ran into mines. ***Breslau*** sank with the loss of 300 men, ***Goeben*** was damaged but escaped. ***Lizard*** was sold for scrap in 1921 to Rees of Llanelli.

HMS Adamant (YN: 0720) was a fleet tender launched on 12 July 1911. Early submarines were without any means for cooking, washing, heating, or accommodation. This prevented their operation at sea without extensive base facilities. The solution was a fleet of support ships which could deploy, providing mobile base facilities. Under the 1910-11 programme the first three ships were laid down; one depot ship for submarine boats and two tenders for submarine boats. ***HMS Adamant*** was one of the latter. She was designed to serve as a tender to the depot ship and escort the submarines on exercises and cruises. She served as a depot ship at Harwich from 1914-15 before moving to the Mediterranean. She was sold in 1932.

The second fleet tender built by Cammell Laird, ***HMS Alecto*** (YN: 0721), was launched in August 1911. Displacing only 935 tons, as opposed to 3,600 of the larger depot ships, both vessels provided workshops, battery charging plants, stores, fuel, torpedoes and accommodation, but on a smaller scale. ***HMS Alecto*** was based at Yarmouth 1914-18 and was sold in 1949.

Floating Dock ***AFD5*** (YN: 0770) also known as the Portsmouth dock was completed in 1912 and could lift 32,000 tons. The picture above shows a test lift of the battleship ***Monarch***. The dock was first based at Invergordon and in the early 1920s it was towed to Portsmouth where it remained until leaving for Alexandria in 1939. Post war, the dock went to Bermuda until 1951 when it was towed to Falmouth. It was sold in 1966 to Maryland Shipbuilding.

The first cruiser built for the Royal Australian Navy, ***HMAS Melbourne*** (YN: 0772) was launched on 30 May 1912 and commissioned on 18 January 1913. Nominally a Town class, the 21 light cruisers were built to a series of designs (Bristol, Weymouth, Chatham, Birmingham & Birkenhead sub-classes). ***Melbourne***, together with ***Sydney*** and ***Brisbane,*** belonged to the Chatham class, which featured a revised armour scheme. While the earlier ships were protected cruisers relying on an internal deep armour deck to protect machinery and magazines, the Chatham group featured a vertical armoured belt. She set sail to Fremantle to be part of the Australian Squadron operating in the Pacific. From 1915 to August 1916 she operated in the West Indies then served in the Grand Fleet. Returning to Cammell Lairds in January 1917 for major engine repairs she returned to Australia in 1919. She was decommissioned in 1925 and returned to the UK in 1928 to be broken up. One of her 6-inch guns has been on display at the Fleet Air Arm Museum.

HMS Audacious (YN: 0775) was laid down in March 1911, as one of four King George V class battleships, and was launched in September 1912, commissioning in 1913. At 23,000 tons her design was a slightly larger Orion class (1909) that featured a main armament of ten 13.5-inch guns and secondary armament of sixteen 4-inch guns. The design was criticised at the time for the weakness of its secondary armament as the majority of foreign battleships were fitted with 5-inch secondary armament. At the beginning of WW1 ***Audacious*** was part of the Grand Fleet, 2nd Battle Squadron.

On 27 October 1914 ***Audacious*** stuck a mine while on gunnery exercises off Lough Swilly in Ireland. Both port and centre engine rooms were flooded and, in order to reduce her list, various compartments on the starboard side were counter flooded. At the time of her striking the mine ***Audacious*** was not at action stations and therefore many watertight doors and hatches remained open. Although these were shut prior to water reaching them, faulty seals around pipes and valves allowed water to spread between compartments, as did broken pipes and hatches that would not close properly. It became impossible to stop the spread of flooding. Attempts were made to take her in tow, including fellow Cammell Laird built ***Exmouth***, however, following a subsequent magazine explosion ***Audacious*** sank some 12 hours after hitting the mine, there were no direct casualties within her ship's company. Her loss was kept secret until after the war.

Officially only decommissioning from Royal Navy service in 2011, ***HMS Caroline*** (YN: 0803) was the longest serving ship, after ***HMS Victory***, currently still in commission. A 'C' class light cruiser she was laid down on 29 January 1914, launched that September and commissioned on 4 December that year making her build less than a year, for which she holds the record for the shortest build of a major warship. Displacing 4,730 tons full load, her armament consisted of two 6-inch guns, eight 4-inch guns and four 21-inch torpedo tubes. ***HMS Caroline*** is one of three surviving Royal Navy ships from WW1 and is the only extant warship from the Battle of Jutland. Later in the war she was fitted with an aircraft flying off platform to allow fighters to attack German Zeppelins crossing the North Sea.

HMS Caroline's sea going career ended in 1922 when she was reduced to reserve, moving to Belfast in 1924 where she was disarmed to become a training ship for the Royal Naval Volunteer Reserve's Ulster Division. During WWII she served as an HQ ship for RN operations from Belfast Harbour and post war returned to her role as training ship. With some £13 million of Lottery grants she is now open to the public in Belfast as part of the National Museum of the Royal Navy.

One of two Town class cruisers ordered in 1914 by Greece and originally named ***Pavlos Kountouriotis***. Based on the Birmingham variation of the Town class, but having 5.5-inch guns as opposed to 6-inch, both vessels were purchased in 1915 for the Royal Navy. ***Pavlos Kountouriotis***, becoming ***HMS Birkenhead*** (YN: 0809), was commissioned in May 1915. She served in the Grand Fleet with the 3rd Light Cruiser Squadron and was present at the Battle of Jutland. In 1921 she was sold for scrap to Cashmore of Newport.

There were seven members of the Lightfoot class flotilla leaders, also known as Marksman class. Cammell Laird built four, starting with ***HMS Kempenfelt*** (YN: 0810), named after the innovative British Rear Admiral Richard Kempenfelt. She was ordered under the 1913-14 Programme. The ships were some 600 tons heavier than normal destroyers, the extra space being for the flotilla commanders and their staff. Laid down in 1914 ***Kempenfelt*** was completed in 1915. Originally all four funnels were the same height but, to reduce smoke interference on the bridge, the first funnel was raised in height on most of the class. She took part in the Battle of Jutland in 1916 and was sold for scrap in 1921.

The second Town class cruiser ordered by Greece, and to be named ***Lambros Katsonis***, ***HMS Chester*** (YN: 0811) was laid down on 7 October 1914, launched on 8 December 1915 and commissioned into the Royal Navy in May 1916. Just three weeks later she fought at Jutland. During the battle ***Chester*** was hit around 18 times, many of the gun crews on deck were killed or badly injured including 16-year old John Travers Cornwell who, despite severe injuries, remained by his gun alone. He later died of his injuries and was posthumously awarded the Victoria Cross. After WW1 the ship went into reserve and was offered back to Greece but they declined and in 1921 she was sold for scrap. The gun manned by John Cornwell VC is now on display at the Imperial War Museum, Lambeth.

Cammell Laird built two members of the Castor class light cruisers, in effect the third group of the 'C' class light cruisers. Seen on her launch day, 28 July 1915, ***HMS Castor*** (YN: 0812) was commissioned in November 1915. She became leader of the 11th Destroyer Flotilla of the Grand Fleet where she was damaged at Jutland with the loss of ten men. Post war she served in the Black Sea during the Russian Civil War. Refitted in 1925 and serving on the China Station she went into reserve in 1930 and was scrapped in 1936. Her sister, ***Constance*** (YN: 0813), was launched on 12 September 1915, commissioned in January 1916, and also fought at Jutland. Post war she served on the China Station until 1930 and was sold for scrap in 1936.

E41 (YN: 0814) was the first of four 'E' class submarines built by Cammell Laird for the Royal Navy, laid down on 26 July 1915, launched the following October she commissioned in February 1916. The 'E' class was a development of the earlier 'D' class. They were larger, better armed and with a greater radius of action. They were intended for operations against warships in the North Sea. The Cammell Laird built vessels were the Group III design of slightly increased size and fitted with a 12-pdr gun on a retractable mounting. On 16 August 1916, ***E41*** sank after colliding with ***E4*** -16 crew were lost. She was raised in 1917 and scrapped in 1922.

Submarine ***E42*** (YN: 0815) was laid down on 23 October 1915 and commissioned in July 1916. In addition to the 12-pdr gun the armament comprised five 18-inch torpedo tubes (two forward, two beam and one stern). When on the surface the range of the vessels was 3,000 miles - submerged at 5 knots the range was 65 miles. The class was largely based at Harwich and on the East coast. ***E42*** was sold for scrap in 1922.

Seen above on launch day, 25 January 1916 ***E45*** (YN: 0816) laid down on 23 October 1915, commissioned in August 1916. She was completed as a minelayer with a reduction of torpedo tubes from five to three. On 15 October 1917 she sank the German submarine ***UC-62*** in the North Sea. She was sold for scrap in September 1922. Conditions in the yard were cramped with Cammell Laird very busy with WW1 work - sister submarine ***E46*** is in the foreground.

Submarine ***E46*** (YN: 0817) was launched on 4 April 1916 and commissioned that October. After the capture of ***UC-2***, a German minelaying submarine in 1915 six of the class were completed as minelayers including ***E41***, ***E45*** and ***E46*** then being built at Cammell Laird. They were fitted with 16 vertical tubes fitted into their saddle tanks that could carry 32 mines, as can be seen in the photograph. A total of 58 'E' class submarines were built by eleven shipyards. ***E46*** was scrapped in 1922.

Lightfoot class flotilla leader destroyer ***HMS Ithuriel*** (YN: 0819) was laid down in 1915. This class of ship were some 600 tons heavier than the earlier 'M' class destroyer they were based upon, to allow space for the flotilla commander plus his staff. Launched on 8 March 1916 she was completed on 2 August 1916. She served with the Grand Fleet throughout WW1 being sold for scrap in Germany in 1921.

Seen in the wet basin ***Gabriel*** (YN: 0818) centre, ***Ithuriel*** (YN: 0819) left, and ***Abdiel*** (YN: 0820). These three ships of the Lightfoot class were ordered under the November 1914 Emergency War Programme and were laid down in 1915 and completed in 1916. ***HMS Gabriel*** was scrapped in 1915.

Seen in the Mersey, with Birkenhead behind, on commissioning, 26 March 1916, ***Abdiel*** (YN: 0820) was completed as a minelayer. The canvas screens aft of her funnels cover two sets of mine rails holding 60 mines in total. During the Battle of Jutland she laid a minefield that damaged the German battleship ***Ostfriesland*** on 4 May 1916. In 1917 she was modified in order to accommodate a further 20 mines and in 1919 she was sent to the Baltic to provide minelaying support to the British intervention in the Russian Civil War. In reserve for much of the 1920s she was sold for scrap in 1936 to Rees of Llanelli.

Repeats of the Lightfoot class, the Parker class comprised six destroyer leaders of whom Cammell Laird built five. ***HMS Parker*** (YN: 0822) was ordered as ***Frobisher*** but her name was changed on launching on 17 June 1916. The class had a displacement of 1,670 tons, were 325 feet long and had a crew of 110. The class had the same basic hull as the Lightfoots but the number of boiler rooms was reduced from three to two allowing the bridge to be moved aft, this resulted in the ships having three instead of four funnels. ***HMS Parker*** became the leader of the 15th Flotilla and served virtually unchanged until sold for scrap in 1921.

An excellent photograph of the Parker class destroyer leader, ***Grenville*** (YN: 0823), on launch day 17 June 1916. She was scrapped in 1931. Her sister ship ***Hoste*** (YN: 0824) laid down on 16 August 1916 and commissioned on 13 November 1916, had a very short career. On 21 December 1916 she suffered a steering gear failure at high speed. She was detached to return to port, escorted by ***Negro***. In heavy seas her rudder jammed again forcing a turn to port. ***HMS Negro***, following astern collided. The collision knocked two depth charges off ***Hoste's*** stern. The subsequent explosion damaged her stern and blew in the bottom of ***Negro's*** hull, causing rapid flooding and subsequent sinking. Attempts to tow ***Hoste*** (by ***Marmion*** and ***Marvel***) failed and she sank 3 hours after the collision. Of the crews, four were lost from ***Hoste*** and 51 from ***Negro***.

HMS Seymour (YN: 0825) was laid down in 1915, launched in 1916 and, on completion, she became leader of the 11th Flotilla. In 1918 she was converted to a minelayer. An innovation fitted to the class was the adoption of the Royal Navy's new director firing system for destroyers and leaders, a more basic version of that on its battleships. Instead of individual gun crews aiming their guns, the crews would be given elevation and bearing. ***HMS Seymour*** was scrapped in 1930. The final Parker class built by Cammell Laird was ***Saumarez*** (YN: 0828), launched on 14 November 1916 and completed on 21 December1916. She was sold for scrap in 1931.

HMS Caledon (YN: 0828) was the lead ship of the Caledon sub-group of the 'C' class light cruiser. She was a slightly larger and improved version of the preceding Centaur sub-group with a more powerful armament comprising five 6-inch guns and eight 21-inch torpedo tubes. She was laid down on 17 March 1916 and launched on 25 November the same year. On commissioning, in March 1917, she saw action in the Second Battle of Heligoland Bight where she was damaged by German shellfire. Still serving with the Home Fleet in the early stages of WWII she participated in the pursuit of German battleships ***Scharnhorst*** and ***Gneisenau***. Converted to an anti-aircraft cruiser between 1942 and 1943 at Chatham Dockyard, she was de-commissioned in April 1945 and sold for scrap in 1948, arriving at Yards of Dover Industries on 14 February.

HMS Valentine (YN: 0829) was a V & W class destroyer of which over 60 were built and was regarded as the best destroyer class produced during WW1. Laid down on 7 August 1916 and completed on 27 June 1917 she entered service with the Grand Fleet. In 1936 she was selected to be modernised as an anti-aircraft escort. She was lost on 5 August 1940, while assisting with the evacuation of Antwerp - one of 16 of the class to be lost during WWII. She was hit by dive bombers and beached with the loss of 31 crew. Partially broken up on site in 1953 sections of her hull can occasionally be seen. ***HMS Valhalla*** (YN: 0830) was the second of the class built by Cammell Laird, laid down in August 1916 and commissioned on 31 July 1917. She was placed in reserve in the 1920s and scrapped around 1931.

The ‘L’ class were enlarged and improved ‘E’ class submarines. They had higher speed and endurance and a better torpedo armament, comprising six 18-inch torpedo tubes (four in the bow and two in broadside mounts) with ten reloads. ***L7*** (YN: 0832) was laid down in May 1916 and commissioned in December 1917. She was initially fitted with a 3-inch gun which was later replaced by a 4-inch mounting. ***L8*** (YN: 0833) was commissioned in March 1918. 73 of the class were planned but only 27 were completed. Both ***L7*** and ***L8*** were initially based in Falmouth, Cornwall, but in 1919 ***L8*** went to Hong Kong. ***L7*** was sold to Hughes Bolckow for scrapping on 26 February 1930 and ***L8*** was sold to John Cashmore Ltd for scrapping on 7 October 1930.

The Scott class destroyer ***Mackay*** (YN: 0850) was laid down on 3 March 1918, launched in December 1918 and commissioned on 19 May 1919. The Scotts were a new class of destroyer leader, built to be flotilla leaders for the V & W classes. Their function was to carry the Flag staff of a destroyer flotilla so were enlarged to carry additional crew, officers and communication equipment. A fifth gun was fitted between the funnels. She was part of the Dunkirk evacuation and unsuccessfully carried out a torpedo attack on the German battleships ***Scharnhorst*** and ***Gneisenau*** as they were emerging into the North Sea after their Channel dash. Present at D-Day she was scrapped in 1947. Class leader ***Scott*** (YN: 0831) was launched in October 1917 but sunk less than a year later (possibly by ***UC-17***) on 15 August 1918 off the Dutch coast. Of other class members built on the Mersey, ***Bruce*** (YN: 0837) was commissioned in 1918 and sunk as a target in 1939 and ***Campbell*** (YN: 0849) was commissioned in 1917 and served throughout WWII before being scrapped in 1947.

HMS Malcolm (YN: 0851), the Scott class destroyer leader was the last of her class to be built. She was laid down on 2 March 1918, launched on 29 May 1919 and commissioned on 14 December 1919. Inter war she served in the 5th Destroyer Flotilla and was later put into reserve as the flotilla leader of the reserve fleet. In 1940 she made eight runs to Dunkirk rescuing British troops. She was badly damaged in the amphibious assault on the port of Algiers in November 1942. She escorted over 60 convoys during WWII and ended her days being sold for scrap in 1945.

The only Royal Navy vessel to be named after the South African city, the 'C' class cruiser ***Capetown*** (YN: 0871) was launched into the Mersey on 28 June 1918. She was fitted out at Pembroke Dock and as hostilities had finished she did not commission until 1922. Much of her service, including WWII, was in the Mediterranean where, on 6 April 1941, she was torpedoed by Italian torpedo boat ***MAS 213***, off Massawa, killing seven of her crew. This resulted in her undergoing a year of repairs in Bombay. In 1944 she became a depot ship at Mulberry 'A' harbour during the Normandy landings and was sold for scrap in 1946.

H33 (YN: 0872) was an 'H' class submarine, laid down in November 1917 and commissioned in May 1919. 34 members of this successful class were ordered with Cammell Laird building ***H33-H40*** but the order was cut back in November 1917 to 24. With a surfaced displacement of 500 tons they were armed with four 21-inch torpedo tubes all located in the bow plus one .303 machine gun. Cammell Laird only built 2 at Birkenhead. In March 1937 the submarine navigated the Gloucester and Sharpness Canal in the company of ***H49***. Still in service at the beginning of WWII, ***H33*** and her remaining sisters were largely used for coastal training until scrapped in 1944. ***H31*** and ***H49***, however, were lost whilst on active service. In the above picture ***H33*** passes Birkenhead.

In effect the 'H' class were modified Holland 602 type submarines designed by The Electric Boat Company based in America. ***H34*** (YN: 0873) was laid down on 20 November 1917 and commissioned (shown above leaving the wet basin) on 10 September 1919. Despite the cramped conditions for her 22 crew the class were popular and ***H34*** served through to the end of WWII, largely in a training role. She was scrapped at Troon in 1945.

The ‘R’ class submarines were ordered in December 1917 with the express purpose of hunting other submarines and were the forerunners of the modern day attack submarine. They were designed to be faster underwater than on the surface, capable of achieving 14 knots submerged. With a streamlined hull, without external ballast tanks or deck guns, they were the fastest submarines of their day. ***R11*** (YN: 0876) is seen above being launched on 16 March 1918 and she was commissioned in August 1919. At the time, the class was considered to be an oddity - their single diesel engine was unable to provide enough charge to provide decent underwater performance and batteries were often charged in port. The bulbous bow contained hydrophone equipment for locating enemy submarines. Their single propeller and circular hulls were features not to be seen again on submarines until after WWII. ***R11*** was sold for scrapping to J. Smith on 21 February 1923.

Twelve 'R' class submarines were ordered but only ten completed. Cammell Laird built just two, the second being ***R12*** (YN: 0877) commissioned in October 1919. The class had a surfaced displacement of 569 tons and were armed with six 18-inch torpedo tubes, all located in the bow, with 18 reloads. The entire class was sent to Killybegs in Donegal to hunt for U-Boats. One is reported to have intercepted a U-Boat in October 1918, but the torpedo that was fired failed to explode. The potential of the class was never realised and ***R12*** was sold for scrapping to J. Smith, with her sister, ***R11***, in February 1923. A single 'R' class, ***R4***, survived until 1934 being used as a fast underwater target at the Portland anti-submarine school. Of interest in the above picture are a number of dazzle painted ships in the background.

One of two Nelson class battleships, ***Rodney*** (YN: 0904) was laid down on 28 December 1922. She was launched by Princess Mary three years later commissioning in November 1927. The class was unique in that all the main armament of nine 16-inch guns were mounted forward of the main superstructure. This was done for two reasons; to allow the entire main armament to be brought to bear on the target at once and also post-Washington Treaty the ships weight had to be below 35,000 tons. This layout with centralised magazines and armour helped achieve this. The three 1,480 ton triple-gun mountings had been ordered for a class of battleship cancelled in the wake of the Washington Treaty. ***HMS Rodney's*** early service was with the Atlantic and Home Fleets. In 1938 she was the first battleship to be equipped with radar.

HMS Rodney is most famous for her action against the German battleship ***Bismarck*** on 27 May 1941. She had been on her way to the USA for a much needed refit when she was called to join the hunt for ***Bismarck*** after she had sunk the battlecruiser ***Hood***. Together with the new battleship ***King George V*** she engaged ***Bismarck*** achieving direct hits from her third salvo fired from 21,000 yards. This initial salvo may have knocked out ***Bismarck's*** gun directors at the beginning of the battle. The battle ended with both battleships firing broadsides from the relatively point black range of two miles. Only minor damage was inflicted on ***Rodney*** by the enemy but the process of firing 340 16-inch shells had caused ***Rodney*** much internal damage. When Dr Robert Ballard discovered the wreck of ***Bismarck***, in 1989, ***Rodney's*** 16-inch shell impacts could clearly be seen, including the hit that disabled the gun directors. Later ***Rodney*** joined Force H and was present at Normandy with her sister ***Nelson***. At the end of the war she was laid up and sold for scrap in 1948.

HMS Phoenix (YN: 0941) was a Parthian class submarine laid down on 23 July 1929, launched the following October and commissioned in February 1931. The class were designed as long range patrol submarines for service in the Far East. She spent her early career on the China station before being sent to the Mediterranean in 1935. Based in Alexandria she took part in the Battle of Calabria where the British attacked the Italian fleet on 8 July 1940. ***HMS Phoenix*** fired torpedoes at two Italian battleships, ***Giulio Cesare*** and ***Conte di Cavour***, but missed both. Eight days later she fired torpedoes at the Italian torpedo boat ***Albatros***, but missed her as well. ***Albatros*** counter-attacked and sank ***Phoenix*** with depth charges. There were no survivors.

Laid down on 11 June 1931, ***Achilles*** (YN: 0983), though intended for the Royal Navy, was in service with the Royal New Zealand Navy throughout WWII. A member of the Leander class light cruisers, of which eight were built, she displaced 9,700 tons fully loaded with a main armament of eight 6-inch guns. The ships also carried one aircraft. Her most famous action was at the Battle of the River Plate in December 1939 in which she, in company with ***Ajax*** and ***Exeter,*** fought the German pocket battleship ***Admiral Graf Spee*** sustaining some damage and six fatalities. ***HMS Achilles*** spent most of the war in the Pacific being returned to the Royal Navy in 1946. Re-commissioned into the Indian Navy in 1948 as ***INS Delhi*** she served until 1978. Her 'Y' turret was gifted to the New Zealand government and is now on display outside Devonport Dockyard, Auckland. In the 1956 film '*Battle of the River Plate*', ***Achilles*** portrays herself.

Of 62 'S' class submarines built, 39 were built by Cammell Laird. ***HMS Sealion*** (YN: 0989) was the first, being laid down on 16 May 1933, launched on 16 March 1934 and commissioned in December of that year. She was a Group II vessel that displaced 670 tons surfaced and 208 feet long. Slightly larger than the Group I vessels, they had a range of 3,800 nautical miles whereas the earlier group had a range of 3,690 nautical miles. During WWII she sank seven ships and damaged another. She unsuccessfully attacked ***U-21*** in 1939 and ***U-74*** in May 1941. She was ordered to attack ***Bismarck*** along with other British submarines prior to ***Dorsetshire*** sinking the crippled battleship with torpedoes. She was scuttled as an ASDIC target off the Isle of Arran on 13 March 1945.

Pictured above in the River Mersey (in the background is the Albert Dock) ***HMS Salmon*** (YN:0990) a Group II 'S' class submarine was laid down on 15 June 1933, launched on 4 April 1934 and commissioned on 8 March 1935, She sank ***U-36*** on 4 December 1939 and shortly after, on 12 December, spotted the German liner ***SS Bremen*** which was not attacked as her captain considered it an illegal target. She was lost, probably sunk by a mine, on 9 July 1940.

Nine Fearless or 'F' class destroyers were planned under the 1932 programme. All nine were laid down in 1933 and launched in 1934. They had a displacement of 1,500 tons, were 329 feet long with an armament of four single mounted 4.7-inch guns, two quadruple 0.5-inch machine guns, two quadruple 21-inch torpedo tubes plus 20 depth charges.The class leader ***Fearless*** (YN: 0992) is seen shortly after launch. Almost identical to the previous Eclipse class, all nine ships formed the 8th Destroyer Flotilla which started WWII in the Home Fleet moving to Force H at Gibraltar in October 1940. On 23 July 1941 both ***Fearless*** and her sister ***Firedrake*** were part of a Malta convoy codename 'Substance' when both were badly damaged by torpedoes dropped by Italian Savoia-Marchetti SM.79 aircraft. 27 crew died. ***HMS Fearless*** was sunk by her sister ***Forester*** to prevent her falling into enemy hands.

Cammell Laird's second 'F' class destroyer, ***Foresight*** (YN: 0993) is seen above on launch day 29 June 1935. On completion she served with the Home Fleet taking a minor role in the Norwegian Campaign of 1940. In mid-1940 she joined Force H at Gibraltar and during her participation in Operation Pedestal on 12 August 1942, supplying Malta with much needed supplies, she was torpedoed by an Italian Savoia-Marchetti SM.79 aircraft . In the attack, ***Foresight*** lost four crew. Despite the loss of her stern she was still able to steam at two knots. Attempts by the destroyer ***Tartar*** to take her in tow failed and the following day she was scuttled at a position north-east of Bone, Algeria.

HMS Hardy (YN: 1008), named after Vice Admiral Sir Thomas Hardy who was the captain of ***HMS Victory*** during the Battle of Trafalgar, was laid down in 1935, launched on 7 April 1936 and commissioned in December of the same year. She was an 'H' class flotilla leader with a displacement of 1,478 tons and an armament consisting of five single mounted 4.7-inch guns, two quadruple mounted 0.5-inch machine guns, two quadruple 21-inch torpedo tubes plus 20 depth charges. In April 1940 she was part of Operation Wilfred which was attempting to lay mines in the Vestfjord to prevent the shipment of Swedish iron ore from Narvik to Germany. With news that German soldiers were being landed at Narvik, ***Hardy*** and her accompanying destroyers were ordered to recapture the town. In the action ***Hardy*** torpedoed the German lead destroyer ***Wilhelm Heidkamp*** and sank a further six vessels. As the British headed for the open sea, however, another five German destroyers attacked causing major damage to ***Hardy*** resulting in the decision to beach the ship and abandon her. Captain Warburton-Lee died shortly after the action and was posthumously awarded the Victoria Cross. The wreck of ***Hardy*** was visible until the 1960s.

HMS Spearfish (YN: 1011) was the last Group II 'S' class submarine built by Cammell Laird. She was laid down on 23 May 1935, launched on 21 April 1936 and completed in December 1936. On 11 April 1940, whilst patrolling in the Kattegat, she torpedoed and damaged the German pocket battleship ***Lützow***, putting her out of action for over a year. On 2 August 1940 ***Spearfish*** was spotted on the surface by ***U-34*** which then attacked and sank her about 180 miles west-southwest of Stavanger. There was only one survivor, Able Seaman William Pester, who was a prisoner of war until 1945 and sadly died shortly after the war in a car accident.

When ordered in 1934, ***Ark Royal*** (YN 1012) was, at £3 million, the most expensive ship built for the Royal Navy. She was laid down in September 1935, launched on 13 April 1937 (as shown above) and commissioned on 16 December 1938. She was the second purpose built aircraft carrier built for the Navy after ***Hermes*** (all other carriers being conversions from capital ships) and the first aircraft carrier to have flight deck and hangars built into the hull giving the ship a very tall appearance. The Washington Treaty had limited her size to 27,000 tons. ***Ark Royal*** had been intended for service in the Far East but spent her whole career in the Home and Mediterranean fleets. Designed for around 70 aircraft, in service she generally embarked around 50 from five squadrons.

HMS Ark Royal had an 800 feet long flight deck, over 100 feet longer than her keel, dry docks in Gibratar and Malta having dictated the length of keel, which resulted in the ship having a distinctive overhang. In her short three years of active service she gained five battle honours, Norway 1940, Spartivento 1940, Mediterranean 1940–41, Bismarck 1941 and Malta Convoys 1941. Famed for surviving many near misses in the Mediterranean her end came on 13 November 1941 while returning to Gibraltar as part of Force H. She was hit by a torpedo fired from ***U-81***. ***HMS Ark Royal's*** machinery spaces were soon flooded which resulted in a complete power loss and heavy list. Attempts were made to tow her to Gibraltar but she was gradually flooding as watertight doors had been left open during the evacuation of her crew and she sank some 30 miles east of Gibraltar with the loss of one man. An enquiry concluded that poor design had led to her loss. She had no back up generators that could have powered the ship's pumps once the main engines had been put out of action.

An interesting stern angle of ***Ark Royal*** in one of Cammell Laird's dry docks. The ship appears to be ready for service and has been in dry dock to allow for painting of her normally submerged hull. Her wreck was discovered by a BBC crew in December 2002, approximately 35 miles from Gibraltar. As she had sunk the hull had broken in two and both sections settled on the sea bed upside down.

HMS Inglefield (YN: 1015) was an 'I' class destroyer leader. She was laid down on 29 April 1936, launched into the Mersey on 15 October that year and commissioned on 25 June 1937. The class were repeats of the earlier 'H' class but had two sets of quintuple 21-inch torpedo tubes instead of quadruple sets. They were also the last flotilla leaders built for the Royal Navy. Early in WWII the after bank of torpedo tubes was removed and replaced with a 12-pdr anti-aircraft gun. The aft funnel was reduced in height by 6 feet to increase the arc of fire from this gun. They were designed to be able to be converted into minelayers.

HMS Inglefield sank the German U-boat ***U-45*** with depth charges on 14 October 1939 when in convoy with her sister vessels ***Ivanhoe*** and ***Intrepid*** and in 1941, while escorting the battleships ***King George V*** and ***Rodney***, was involved in the action that sank ***Bismarck***. She was part of the escort for the first convoy to the Russia, along with ***Victorious*** and then ***Argus***. ***HMS Inglefield*** remained with the Home fleet until July 1943 when she was transferred to the Mediterranean where her first major action in July 1943 was the invasion of Sicily. On 25 February 1944, however, she was hit and sunk by a German HS 293 glider bomb off Anzio while protecting the Allied landings. 35 crew died.

ARA Misiones (YN: 1021) was a member of the six strong Buenos Aires class of destroyers built in the UK for Argentina. They were based on the British 'G' class but modified to suit Argentine requirements. Named after territories in the Argentine Republic, all were laid down in 1936. ***ARA Misiones*** was launched in September 1937 and commissioned on 5 September 1938, serving until 1971. To the left, sistership ***ARA Santa Cruz*** nears completion.

A fantastic picture of ***ARA Santa Cruz*** (YN: 1022) being towed into Cammell Laird's wet basin, passing ***Ark Royal*** on her launch day, 3 November 1937. Entering service in September 1938 ***ARA Santa Cruz*** served until 1973 being updated post war with radar and air cooled Bofors guns (as opposed to the standard water-cooled variants) that were only fitted to Argentine and Swedish warships.

The Dale class fleet tanker ***RFA Aldersdale*** (YN: 1025) was ordered in 1936 by The British Tanker Company. She was purchased by the Admiralty whilst under construction. She was launched on 7 July 1937 and commissioned two months later. Whilst on Arctic convoy PQ17, the Russian-bound convoy was ordered to scatter fearing a German attack. Of the 35 merchant ships, 24 were lost. ***RFA Aldersdale*** was bombed by German aircraft on 5 July 1942, abandoned and later torpedoed by ***U-457***.

Originally intended to be named ***King Edward VIII***, the King's abdication in 1938 resulted in the ship being laid down on 1 January 1937 as ***Prince of Wales*** (YN: 1026). She was launched in May 1939 and completed in March of 1941. Displacing 43,780 tons with a length of 745 feet her main armament comprised ten 14-inch guns mounted in three turrets, a quadruple mount fore and aft plus a twin mount forward in 'B' position. Secondary armament was sixteen 5.25-inch guns in eight twin mountings. She could also carry four Supermarine Walrus seaplanes that were launched from a midships mounted catapult. Her first action was on 22 May 1941 with the battlecruiser ***Hood*** against the German battleship ***Bismarck***. At the time her crew also included shipyard workers as the main armament still required further work due to the regular jamming of the machinery. ***HMS Prince of Wales*** scored two hits on ***Bismarck*** but in the action ***Hood*** was lost and ***Prince of Wales*** damaged to a point where she disengaged the enemy after a ten hour pursuit.

HMS Prince of Wales, following repairs at Rosyth after the ***Bismarck*** encounter, carried Prime Minister Winston Churchill in secret to meet American President Franklin D. Roosevelt in August 1941 at Placentia Bay, Newfoundland. In September 1941 she was sent to Singapore to join the Far East fleet, joining with the battlecruiser ***Repulse***, to become Force Z. On 10 December 1941 they were attacked off Kuantan in the South China Sea by Japanese aircraft and, lacking any RAF air cover, both ships were sunk by bombs and torpedoes. 327 men from ***Prince of Wales*** were lost. In 2002 her bell was recovered, with the permission of the Ministry of Defence, and is on display at the Liverpool Maritime Museum at the Albert Docks. There have been reports that the wreck has been the subject of illegal scrap recovery in recent years. (*Image: Syd Goodman Collection*)

What is probably the most tragic incident in the history of Cammell Laird, was the loss of the 'T' class submarine ***Thetis*** (YN: 1027). On 1 June 1939 ***Thetis*** headed out into Liverpool Bay to carry out diving trials. Onboard were 103 people, almost doubling her normal crew. Many of the extra people were Cammell Laird workers. The first attempt to dive failed, the boat being too light. Whilst trying to resolve the problem it was assumed that the inner door of a torpedo tube was opened, whilst a defective indicator showed that the outer door was shut. It was open and the resulting influx of sea water into the submarine caused a near vertical dive. Although the stern was 18 feet out of the water the escape hatch was below water and only four men escaped alive. An attempt to tow ***Thetis*** resulted in the submarine sinking. She was recovered a few months later, repaired and renamed ***Thunderbolt***. She was sunk in the Mediterranean on 14 March 1943 by an Italian depth charge. As a result of her loss in 1939 the 'Thetis clip' was introduced whereby the inner torpedo tube door could be opened slightly to check for water before being fully opened.(*Image: Ken Kelly Collection*)

Cammell Laird built seven of the 53 'T' class submarines completed. They had a remarkable bow salvo of ten torpedoes, eight bow tubes and two amidships, angled out from the casing abreast of the bridge. ***HMS Trident*** (YN: 1028) was laid down on 12 January 1937, launched in December 1938 and completed in October 1939.The ten torpedo tubes were 21-inch and she also had a 4-inch gun. Displacement was 1,090 tons surfaced and 1,570 tons submerged. The submarine had a very eventful war. Her most famous action was against the German cruisers ***Prinz Eugen*** and ***Admiral Hipper***. on 23 February 1942. She fired seven torpedoes at them, causing damage to ***Admiral Hipper***. For much of the war the submarine had a young reindeer doe on board that had been a gift from the Russians in 1941. The animal adapted to submarine life well but eventually it grew too big for the boat and was removed and sent to a zoo. ***HMS Trident*** spent the latter period of WWII in the Far East before being scrapped in 1946.

HMS Dido (YN: 1033) was the lead ship of the Dido class light cruisers, laid down on 20 October 1937 and launched on 18 July 1939. The class was designed primarily as a fleet anti-aircraft escort for which purpose the ships were fitted with ten 5.25-inch guns mounted in five twin turrets that could also engage surface targets. The hull and machinery were based on the Arethusa class with a length of 512 feet and displacement of 7,000 tons full load. Commissioned in 1940, her service included the Mediterranean and Arctic convoys. She was bombed whilst operating off Crete, requiring repairs in the USA. On 8 May 1945, ***Dido*** was en route to Copenhagen in Denmark. At one point during the journey, the ship was approached by a lone German aircraft. The cruiser fired one shot and the plane flew away - it was VE day and that was the last shot fired in the Second World War in Europe. In the 1950s she was flagship of the reserve fleet before being sold for scrap to T.W. Ward in 1957.

HMS Taku (YN: 1036), a 'T' class submarine, was laid down on 18 November 1937. She was launched on 20 May 1939 - pictured above as tugs tow her into the wet basin for fitting out - and was commissioned in January 1940. She served in Home Waters and the Mediterranean, sinking over ten ships. In April 1944 she and ***Venturer*** were tasked with entering the Skagerrak. Royal Navy submarines had not operated in the area since 1940 and entry to the operating area would require transitting a dense minefield. ***HMS Taku*** went first at depth to penetrate below the minefield. After five hours there was a heavy explosion overhead causing flooding in the gun tower and minor leaks. She reversed course and exited the minefield. Post-war it was discovered that the Germans had heavily reinforced the minefields and deployed a new type of mine with antennae down the mooring wire to detonate if anything touched it. She was sold for scrap in 1946.

The first 'T' class Group I submarine to enter service with a name, ***HMS Talisman*** (YN: 1040) was launched on a snowy 29 January 1940, commissioning that June. Her short career was largely spent in the Mediterranean, sinking the Vichy-French passenger ship ***Théophile Gautier*** and the Italian merchant ***Calitea***. ***HMS Talisman*** had been sent to the Mediterranean in August 1942 as a reinforcement. On her way to Gibraltar she was attacked and damaged by a RAF Sunderland flying boat resulting in her spending the best part of a month under repair at Gibraltar. She sailed on 10 September 1942 carrying supplies to Malta, and reported a U-boat off Philippeville, Algeria, five days later. Failing to arrive at Malta she was declared missing on 18 September. It is thought she may have hit a mine or been sunk by Italian forces with the loss of all hands.The picture shows the torpedo tubes uncovered which is very unusual.

Another Dido class cruiser built by Cammell Laird for the Royal Navy, ***Charybdis*** (YN: 1041) was laid down in November 1939. Her intended main armament of ten 5.25-inch guns had to be substituted by eight 4.5-inch guns in four turrets as her intended 5.25-inch turrets were identical to the secondary armament of the King George V class and the battleships took priority. Her service commenced with the Home Fleet in December 1941 and she was transferred to Force H, based at Gibraltar, in April 1942. ***HMS Charybdis*** took part in some of the fiercest battles including Operation Pedestal. Her end came in October 1943, after she had returned to the Home Fleet when she was torpedoed by German Elbing-class boats ***T-27*** and ***T-33***, sinking within 30 minutes with a loss of 400 of her 480 crew.

Lead ship of the Hunt class, ***Atherstone*** (YN: 1043) was laid down on 8 June 1939, launched on 12 December 1939 and completed in March 1940. During testing it was found that, due to a design error, the class were top heavy and thus unstable, resulting in ***Atherstone*** having her superstructure and funnel reduced in height. In September 1940 she was hit by two bombs whilst on escort duty in the English Channel. She was involved in Operation Chariot during March 1942, sailing from Falmouth with the explosive-filled ***Campbeltown*** with the aim of destroying the Normandie dock at St Nazaire by ramming the dock with the ***Campbeltown***, which, after allowing time for her crew to escape would explode denying the Germans the use of the dock for the German battleship ***Tirpitz***. Decommissioned at the end of the war she was in reserve until 1953 before being broken up at Glasgow in 1957.

The second of the Hunt class built by Cammell Laird was ***HMS Berkeley*** (YN: 1044) launched on a wintery January day in 1940 and completed by June of that year. Stability was still an issue which resulted in the class being fitted with Denny fin stabilizers, which were only of limited use and occupied valuable space. After the fall of France she evacuated British Embassy staff and she participated in the unsuccessful attempt to intercept the German battleships ***Scharnhorst*** and ***Gneisenau*** during the Channel Dash. During the Dieppe raid on 19 August 1942 ***Berkeley*** was badly damaged by two bombs dropped by German Focke-Wulf Fw-190 aircraft, breaking her keel and killing 13 of her crew . With no chance of her recovery she was scuttled by torpedoes fired from ***Albrighton***.

HMS Argonaut (YN: 1047) was one of 16 Dido class anti-aircraft cruisers. She was laid down in November of 1939 and launched (pictured above) on 6 September 1941. Following completion in September 1942 she joined the 10th Cruiser Squadron of the Home Fleet but moved to Gibraltar in November to be part of Force H. She was badly damaged by Italian torpedoes on 14 December which damaged the bow and blew off the stern, requiring repairs in the USA. Early in 1944 she had returned to the UK where further work included new radars and the removal of 'Q' turret, the upper forward turret, in order to reduce top weight. Shore bombardment during D-Day was followed by service in the Far East including troop repatriation. She returned to Portsmouth in 1946 to be de-commissioned. After some years in reserve she was sold for scrap in 1955.

HMS Blencathra (YN: 1048) was a Type II Hunt laid down in November 1939 and commissioned in December 1940. Type II Hunts were two feet wider, had a revised bridge structure and could carry double the number of depth charges as the Type I. Much of ***Blencathra's*** service was in the Mediterranean where she participated in the landings at Sicily and Salerno and also assisted in the destruction of ***U-233*** and ***U-450***. Back in Home Waters she protected the Normandy landings at Utah Beach. With armament removed she became a target ship in October 1945, a role she performed until 1948 when she decommissioned, being scrapped by T.W. Ward in 1957.

The Royal Navy's 'T' class were the first submarines to be named rather than just numbered. ***HMS Thrasher*** (YN: 1050) was laid down on 14 November 1939, launched on 28 November 1940 and commissioned in May 1941. A Group II boat, she had the external bow torpedo tubes moved 7 feet backwards to improve sea keeping, the midships tubes moved further aft behind the conning tower to allow rear firing and the addition of a stern torpedo tube giving eleven tubes in total. In February 1942, while attacking merchant ships off Crete, ***Thrasher*** surfaced to find two unexploded bombs in the forward casing. Lieutenant Peter Scawen Watkinson Roberts and Petty Officer Thomas William Gould removed the first one without too much difficulty, but the second was lying in a very confined space and they had to approach it lying full length. Gould lay on his back with the bomb in his arms while Roberts dragged him along by the shoulders. It took almost an hour before the men could drop the bomb over the side saving the ship. Both men received the Victoria Cross for their action. Around 20,000 tons of shipping was sunk while ***Thrasher*** was in the Mediterranean. She was scrapped in 1947.

HMS Thorn (YN: 1051) was another short-lived 'T' class submarine. Laid down in January 1940, launched on 18 March 1941, she was completed in August 1941 and commenced operations in the Mediterranean. Early successes included the German tanker ***Campina***, the Italian tanker ***Ninuccia*** and the Italian submarine ***Medusa***. It is thought that ***Thorn*** had orders to proceed to an area off Cape Matapan but on the way she met the Italian destroyer ***Papa*** off Gavdos Island, the southernmost of the Greek islands. She was sighted, depth charged and sunk with the loss of the entire crew. A final 'T' class boat, ***Tempest*** (YN: 1052), was sunk by another Italian torpedo boat ***Circe*** on 13 February 1942 in the Gulf of Taranto, 23 crew were picked up.

Another Type II Hunt, ***Badsworth*** (YN: 1055) was laid down in March 1940, launched in May 1941 and commissioned in November that year. Her early career included service in the NW Approaches, West Africa and on the Arctic convoys. While on convoy escorting duties, in August 1941, she was badly damaged by a mine on entering Grand Harbour, Malta, causing major structural damage. Temporary repairs were made at Malta before she returned to service in December 1942. She was loaned to Norway in August 1944 becoming ***HNoMS Arendal*** and was purchased outright at the end of hostilities. In September 1945 she had the duty of returning the remains of 400 Norwegian servicemen to Norway who had been killed while in service in the United Kingdom. Post war she was used as a destroyer escort being reclassified as a frigate in 1956. Following a period as a cadet training ship she was removed from service in 1961.

A Batch III 'S' class submarine, ***Saracen*** (YN: 1059) was laid down on 16 July 1940, launched on 16 February 1942 and commissioned in June 1942. Her original number was P213, to which her crew objected, as it was considered unlucky. Upon completion she was numbered P247, still adding up to 13! She sank ***U-335*** in the North Sea and whilst in the Mediterranean she accounted for seven enemy ships. On 13 August 1943, whilst on patrol off Bastia, ***Saracen*** was spotted by the Italian corvettes ***Minerva*** and ***Euterpe*** which attacked with depth charges. She remained submerged as the commanding officer did not want to scuttle the boat on Friday 13th! She surfaced at 0200 on Saturday 14 August, the crew scuttling her to avoid her capture. In June 2015 her wreck was discovered in 1,000 feet of water.

The ‘R’ destroyer ***Raider*** (YN: 1064) was ordered under the 1940 programme to form the 4th Emergency Flotilla comprising eight ships. Launched on 1 April 1942 she entered service that November being assigned to the 11th Destroyer Flotilla, Eastern Fleet, and after work-up spent three months on anti-submarine patrols and escorting cruisers covering Arctic convoys. In February 1943 she left the Clyde for the Eastern Fleet and reached as far as Kilindini before being ordered back to the Mediterranean to cover Operation Husky and the Salerno Landings. In January 1944 she finally reached Trincomalee to join the Far East Fleet where, in 1945, she participated in Operation Zipper, the reoccupation of Malaya. She was decommissioned on 1 October 1945 at Devonport but recommissioned in May 1946 to act as a tender to aircraft carriers in the Mediterranean, which included recovering aircrew from landing or take-off accidents. In reserve at Devonport in 1948, in 1949 she commenced a two year refit after which she was sold to India becoming ***INS Rana***. She was finally decommissioned on 30 September 1971.

The second 'R' class destroyer built by Cammell Laird, ***Rapid*** (YN: 1065) was laid down on 16 May 1941 and launched on 16 July 1942. She was assigned to the Eastern Fleet 11th Destroyer Flotilla and her war service included operations in the Indian and Pacific Oceans. After the war in 1946 she was commissioned as an Air Training Target Ship. Between June 1951 and October 1953 she was totally rebuilt as a Type 15 Frigate by Alex Stephen on the Clyde, but then spent the period 1954-1965 in reserve at Portsmouth. In 1966 she was allocated to the shore establishment ***HMS Caledonia*** to assist in the sea training of engine room artificers. The ship was used for short trips from Rosyth Dockyard to give artificers first hand experience. By June 1974 she was listed for disposal and a couple of months later became a target ship based at Pembroke Dock. ***HMS Rapid*** was sunk by a Cammell Laird built submarine, ***Onyx***, which fired two torpedoes at her in 1981.

A Type III Hunt class destroyer, ***Aldenham*** (YN: 1077) was laid down in August 1940, launched the following August and commissioned in February 1942, becoming the first RN ship to carry the name. The Type IIIs were fitted with a bank of twin 21-inch torpedo tubes so that the ships could be used in offensive operations against enemy shipping. To compensate for the additional weight it was necessary to reduce the number of twin 4-inch gun mountings from three to two. In March she was involved in the sinking of ***U-587*** and in 1943 she participated in the Italian landings at Sicily and Salerno. She became the last Royal Navy destroyer to be sunk in WWII when on 14 December 1944 she struck a mine in the Adriatic off Pag Island. 122 of 189 of her crew were lost.The wreck was located in 1999 and is a designated war grave.

HMS Belvoir (YN: 1078), a Type III Hunt class escort destroyer, was ordered on 4 July 1940 as part of the 1940 War Emergency Programme. She was laid down on 14 October 1940, launched in November 1941 and completed in March 1942. Initial service was on the Arctic convoys. She took part in Operation Husky, the Salerno landings and, on 13 November 1943 rescued 109 survivors from ***Dulverton*** which had sustained extensive damage in an attack by a glider bomb during the defence of Leros. She spent the remainder of the war based at Malta. Post war she was reduced to reserve at Portsmouth where she remained until transferred to Harwich in 1950. Returning to Portsmouth in 1952 she was placed on the disposal list and in 1957 was sold for scrapping to P.W. MacLellan, Bo'ness, where she arrived on 21 October 1957.

HMS Glaisdale (YN: 1081) was transferred to Norway on 23 December 1941, launched on 5 January 1942 and was completed on 12 June 1942. She served under Norwegian command and was deployed under Royal Navy control with a British flotilla. On 15 November she picked up 312 survivors from the British troop transport ***Ettrick*** that had been torpedoed and sunk by the German U-boat ***U-155*** 120 miles northwest of Gibraltar. Badly damaged by a mine during the Normandy landings of 1944 she was paid off in August 1944 being returned to the Royal Navy who in turn laid her up at Hartlepool. In August 1946 she was sold to Norway, renamed ***HNoMS Narvik***, and refitted at Chatham. Reclassified as a frigate in 1956, she remained in commission until 1962.

Some 86 Hunt class destroyers were built for the Royal Navy of which 14 went on to serve with other navies. ***HMS Eskdale*** (YN: 1082) was one of three that served with the Norwegian Navy. She served as ***HNoMS Eskdale*** and was laid down at Cammell Laird on 18 January 1941. Launched in March 1942 she was completed in July of 1942. On 14 April 1943, along with sister-ship ***Glaisdale***, and five trawlers they were escorting Channel Convoy PW232. They came under attack 12 miles east of the Lizard by E-Boats of the 3rd German Flotilla. ***HNoMS Eskdale*** was hit by two torpedoes fired by ***S-90*** and disabled. She sank in position 5003N 0546W after being hit by a further torpedo from ***S-112*** with the loss of 25 of her crew. She lies in 195 feet of water and is accessible to scuba divers.

One of eight 'S' class destroyers ordered in 1941, ***Scorpion*** (YN: 1094) was laid down the same year, launched in August 1942 and commissioned the following May. Later ships were fitted with lattice masts to cater for additional electronic equipment and they were optimised for Arctic operations. The entire class served with the Home Fleet where they formed the 23rd Destroyer Flotilla. With three of her sisters, ***Scorpion*** took part in the Battle of North Cape where the destroyer force fired torpedoes at the German battlecruiser ***Scharnhorst*** scoring four hits which slowed her down allowing the battleship ***Duke of York*** and the accompanying cruiser force to sink her. She was present at Normandy in 1944 and in October 1945 she was sold to the Dutch Navy becoming ***Kortenaer***. During 1958 and 1959 she was converted to a fast frigate with 4 x 4.7-inch guns, 6 x 40mm guns plus 8 x 21-inch torpedo tubes. A flight deck was also fitted between the funnel and 'X' turret. She was sold for scrap in 1962 arriving at Ghent for demolition on 18 July 1963.

Cammell Laird's second 'S' class destroyer was ***Scourge*** (YN: 1095) which was laid down 26 June 1941, launched on 8 December 1941and completed in July 1943. The 'S' class was a repeat of the earlier 'R' class of which Cammell Laird had built two. She was at sea during the Battle of North Cape in 1943, escorting the Russia-bound Arctic convoy JW 55B. She took no part in the fighting and in August 1945 was reduced to care and maintenance at Portsmouth. She was then refitted and tropicalised prior to being transferred, along with her sister ***Scorpion***, to the Royal Netherlands Navy, becoming ***Evertsen***. She served with the British Pacific Fleet on North Borneo Patrols until 1947 and saw action in Korea. In 1957 she was converted to a fast frigate at Rijkswerk, Willenstaad. She arrived for scrapping at Hendrik Ido Ambacht in July 1963.

A total of sixty-two 'S' class submarines were constructed over a period of 15 years of which Cammell Laird built thirty-five. ***HMS Stubborn*** (YN: 1096) was laid down on 9 October 1941, launched on 11 November 1941 and commissioned in February 1943. A Group III boat, she was, at 715 tons surfaced, 30 tonnes heavier than the preceding Group IIs and at 217 feet long was slightly longer, which allowed for a greater fuel load, extending her surfaced range to 6,000 nautical miles. She spent most of the war in home waters. She was once attacked north west of Namsos, Folda Fjord and ended up diving to a depth of 500 feet, some 200 feet below her design maximum, after her hydroplanes jammed in the full dive position. She survived this incident, though she required extensive repairs. Lt Cdr Alistair Mars observed her at Devonport and said: "*I myself, then busy with the fitting-out of **Thule**, met Duff after arrival and examined **Stubborn** in the drydock. She gave the impression of a skeleton's chest; for her ribs protruded, whilst between them, her steel plates had been pressed inwards to form concave curves, this bizarre effect providing unforgettable tribute to the workmanship of the men who built her.*" ***HMS Stubborn*** survived the Second World War and was sunk on 30 April 1946 as an ASDIC target off Malta. This picture clearly shows the position of her aft external torpedo tube.

HMS Surf (YN: 1097), a Group III 'S' class submarine was launched on 10 December 1942. The boat served in the Mediterranean and the Far East during WWII. Whilst in the Mediterranean she damaged the German auxiliary patrol vessel ***GA 54 / Chiaros*** and sank the German merchantman ***Sonia***. On transfer to the Far East, she sank a small Japanese tug and a barge and laid mines in the Strait of Malacca. ***HMS Surf*** survived the war and was sold on 28 October 1949. She arrived at Faslane in July 1950 for breaking up.

The 'T' class were a follow-on to the 'S' class except that they were not fitted for Arctic operations. ***HMS Teazer*** (YN: 1099) was laid down on 20 October 1941, launched on 7 January 1943, completing in September of that year. The class formed the 24th Destroyer Flotilla and was initially sent to the Mediterranean until late 1944 when they sailed to join the British Pacific Fleet. In reserve at Devonport from 1946 to 1953 she was then converted, at Mountstuart Dry Docks, to a Type 16 frigate and, in January 1959, replaced ***Grenville*** in the 2nd Training Squadron. The Type 16 frigate conversion was a far more limited conversion than the Type 15s which were complete rebuilds. Type 16 retained most of the structure but had the armament reduced to one twin 4-inch gun mount, 7 x 40mm, two Squid anti-submarine mortars and a quadruple set of 21-inch torpedo tubes. She was transferred to the disposal list in September 1961 and arrived in Dalmuir in August 1965 for scrapping.

The second 'T' class built by Cammell Laird was ***Tenacious*** (YN: 1100), laid down 3 December 1941, launched on 24 March 1943 and commissioned on 30 October. She was initially named ***Tempest***. Wartime service in the Mediterranean and Pacfic was followed by three years in reserve at Devonport becoming, in 1949, a target ship for the 3rd Submarine Flotilla at Rothesay. Between 1951 and 1952 she was converted into a Type 16 frigate at Rosyth and on completion operated with the 3rd Training Squadron at Portsmouth and Londonerry before entering reserve at Rosyth in July 1954. Following a brief reactivation in 1955 she returned to reserve at Rosyth until moving to Barrow in November 1956 and to Devonport in September 1963. On 29 June 1965 she was sold for breaking up at Troon.

The Modified Black Swan class sloop ***Cygnet*** (YN: 1101) was launched on 28 July 1942 and completed that December. The class of 12 original Black Swan and 25 Modified Black Swans, were very successful anti-submarine escorts, accounting for some 29 U-boats sunk during WWII. They had a displacement of 1,350 tons, length of 299 feet and an armament of 6 x 4-inch guns, 10 x 20mm guns and 110 depth charges. ***HMS Cygnet*** survived the war and, after a period in reserve at Devonport, served in the Fishery Protection Squadron from 1948. In 1951 she served in the Mediterranean with the 5th Frigate Flotilla, moving to the 2nd Frigate Flotilla a year later before going into reserve at Chatham in 1954. Sold to Bisco in 1956, she arrived at Rosyth on 16 March for demolition.

HMS Kite (YN: 1102) was the second Modified Black Swan class sloop built by Cammell Laird, being launched on 12 October 1942 and commissioned the following March. For some of her career she was based across the river at the Gladstone Dock. She was once commanded by the famous U-boat hunter Captain Frederick John Walker and in 1944 participated in the famous '*Six in One Trip*' where, on one patrol, six U-boats (***U-592***, ***U-762***, ***U-734***, ***U-238***, ***U-424*** and ***U-264***) were sunk by ***Kite*** and accompanying ships. On 21 August 1944, while escorting Russian convoy JW-51, she was torpedoed by ***U-344*** as she had slowed to untangle her 'Foxers' (anti-acoustic torpedo noise makers, towed astern). She sank 220 miles south west of Bear Island. Only nine of her crew survived the sinking and subsequent immersion in the freezing Arctic water, being rescued by ***Keppel***.

A member of the 7th Emergency Flotilla, the 'U' class destroyer ***Ulysses*** (YN: 1103) was laid down on 14 March 1942. The class were a follow-on to the Savage class and the 7th-11th Flotillas were repeats of the 5th and 6th but without the 4-inch HA mount, which were not fitted for Arctic service. Launched on 22 April 1943 and commissioned on 23 December 1943, her wartime service started with the 25th Destroyer Flotilla, Home Fleet, which included some escorting of Arctic convoys before becoming part of the British Pacific Fleet in March 1946. She returned to Devonport in 1946 to be placed in reserve. Conversion to Type 15 frigate followed in 1954-1955 and she recommissioned as a member of the 6th Frigate Squadron in the Meditteranean/Home Fleet. ***HMS Ulysses*** participated in Operation Grapple, the nuclear tests on Christmas Island, in 1958. She was reduced to reserve in 1959 with her crew transferring to commission ***Yarmouth*** in 1961. She replaced ***Petard*** as Plymouth training ship and then became a Dartmouth cadet training ship. Placed in unmaintained reserve in 1962 she was sold to Messrs Davies & Carr Ltd in October 1969 for scrap. In the photograph the main armament is trained towards the camera, a common practice when new ships were photographed. It is believed that it was done to disguise the calibre of the guns from prying eyes.

The final 'U' class destroyer built by Cammell Laird, ***Undaunted*** (YN: 1104) was laid down on 8 September 1942, launched on 19 July 1943 and commissioned in March the following year. She had a busy wartime career starting with escorting the carrier group involved in attacking the German battleship ***Tirpitz*** in the Norwegian Altenfjord. During operations on D-Day she transported General Dwight D. Eisenhower back from Normandy to Portsmouth and then served in the Mediterranean. In reserve from 1946 to 1951 she was converted into a Type 15 frigate, commissioning into the 2nd Training Squadron in July 1954 for service as a trials vessel with the Admiralty Underwater Weapons Establshment (AUWE) at Portland. In 1959 a helicopter pad was fitted for trials of the Saunders Roe P531 light helicopter that in service became the Westland Wasp. Paying off in 1973 she was used as a target for Exocet missiles fired by the County class guided missile destroyer ***Norfolk*** and was finally sunk by torpedoes from the submarine ***Swiftsure*** in 1978 off Gibraltar.

Ordered by the Ministry of War Transport and operated by the British Tanker Company, now BP, ***MV Empire MacColl*** (YN: 1106) was a Merchant Aircraft Carrier (MAC ship) of the Empire MacKay class. These were oil tankers that had been converted to carry a small number of aircraft primarily to escort convoys. The flight deck was built over her upper deck allowing the ship to retain her freighting capacity. Post war she was rebuilt as a normal oil tanker being renamed ***British Pilot*** in 1946. After commercial service she was scrapped in 1962.

HMS Stoic (YN: 1107) was laid down on 18 June 1942, launched on 19 April 1943 and commissioned in June 1943. She spent most of WWII in the Far East where she sank ten Japanese vessels and also bombarded warehouses and fuel tanks at Jangka Island. Post war ***Stoic*** which had a rivetted hull and a sister, ***Supreme***, which had an all-welded hull, were used to carry out deep diving trials. Held by lifting craft, they were lowered until their hulls were crushed by the pressure of the sea. This finally occurred at over 250 feet below their maximum operational diving depths. She was sold in July 1950 to be broken up at Dalmuir.

HMS Storm (YN: 1109) was laid down on 23 June 1942, launched in May 1943 and commissioned in July that year. Her captain was Edward Young who had been in publishing before the war. In 1952 he published a book '*One Of Our Submarines*' which describes his war experience, largely on ***Storm***, and gives an excellent insight into service life on a wartime Royal Navy submarine. After initial service in the Arctic, ***Storm*** was sent to the Far East to the Malacca Straits between Malaya and Sumatra, both then occupied by the Japanese. Operating later from Australia she briefly held the record for the longest 'S' class patrol of 37 days. She returned home in April 1945 and was scrapped in 1949.

Further follow-ons to the 'S' class, the 'Z' class were ordered to form the 10th Flotilla of the Emergency War Programme. ***HMS Zambesi*** (YN: 1117), the only Royal Navy ship to bear the name, was, laid down in December 1942, launched the following November and completed in July 1944. Her war service mainly involved escorting Arctic convoys prior to being placed in reserve at Devonport from 1946-50. She was refitted at Gibraltar in 1948 and in the early 1950s served as target ship for the 3rd Submarine Flotilla at Rothesay. She arrived Devonport to decommission on 10 December 1952 and, after de-storing, left Plymouth in tow of ***Antic*** to be laid up at Penarth. It had been proposed to convert her to a Type 15 frigate at Cammell Laird but this was cancelled. In 1956 she was offered to Peru but the sale fell through and she arrived at T.W. Ward, Briton Ferry for breaking up on 12 December 1959.

Cammell Laird's second 'Z'class destroyer was ***Zealous*** (YN: 1118). She was laid down in May 1943, launched on 28 February 1944 and commissioned in October 1944. War service included escorting Arctic convoys and serving with the Home Fleet until going into the reserve fleet at Devonport in 1947. Transferred to Israel in July 1955 she became ***Eilat***. She was sunk off Port Said by three Egyptian-fired Styx missiles on 21 October 1967, being one of the first casualties of surface launched anti-ship missiles. Of her crew of around 200, 47 died and 100 were wounded. Torpedo tubes removed from ***Eilat*** prior to the attack are on display at the Clandestine Immigration and Naval Museum, Haifa.

What is possibly one of the most famous Royal Navy warships, ***Ark Royal*** (YN: 1119) was one of four Audacious class aircraft carriers ordered for the Royal Navy. Laid down on 3 May 1943 as ***Irresistible***, her name was changed just before her launch on the 3 May 1950 to ***Ark Royal*** in order to perpetuate the name as the previous ***Ark Royal*** had been sunk in 1941. Launched by the then Queen Elizabeth, the Queen Mother continued her association with the ship throughout her career.

Just after her launch, tugs guide ***Ark Royal*** towards the fitting out quay with wood from the slipway floating in the foreground. It was five years until she commissioned in 1955, with changes to her design causing much of the delay. This was a period of rapid development in naval aviation. A ship originally designed to operate propeller driven aircraft such as the Sea Fury would have to be adapted for much heaver, faster jet aircraft, such as the Sea Vixen, that were coming into service in the late 1950s. One such change was the waist deck edge lift which was removed from ***Ark Royal*** in 1961. Popular with American carriers, side lifts have made a return on the current Queen Elizabeth class but this time not on the flight line.

HMS Ark Royal is towed into Cammell Laird's fitting-out basin. Her career of 24 years was relatively short by comparison to the later Invincible class which averaged just over 28 years each (***Illustrious*** reached 32 years service). Of her 24 years service about half were spent in refit. In her final 1967-70 refit her flight deck was upgraded to allow for operation of the new McDonnell Douglas Phantom aircraft. She was also fitted for, but not with, four Seacat launchers, leaving her with no defensive armament. There had been plans to withdraw her in 1975 but the Royal Navy managed to keep her in service until late 1978 by which time, not only was she difficult to maintain, she was also crew intensive with over 2,000 and the RAF was desperate for the Fleet Air Arm's Buccaneer and Phantom aircraft. After a year laid up she was towed to Scotland for scrapping where, by 1983, there were still large sections of her visible. An anchor is on display at the Fleet Air Arm Museum, Yeovilton and another is on display in Plymouth.

The Battle class destroyer ***Hogue*** (YN: 1124) was laid down in January 1943. Her name was taken from the Battle of La Hogue, fought between the British and French in 1692. The Battle class were built with heavy anti-aircraft gunnery based on WWII experience which showed that for one day on which a destroyer fired her guns at another ship she probably fired them at aircraft 20 times. Armament comprised 2 x twin HA/LA 4.5-inch gun turrets forward, 1 x 4-inch gun, 4 x twin 40mm, 4-6 single 40mm, 2 x quadruple 21-inch torpedo tubes and 2 x depth charge rails. Launched in April 1944 she was commissioned into the British Pacific Fleet the following July where she remained until going into reserve in 1947 at Devonport. She remained there for ten years. In 1957 she was refitted and returned to service with the 1st Destroyer Squadron on 21 May 1957. She served in the first Cod War two years later alongside the now preserved destroyer ***Cavalier***. She participated in the filming of the movie *Sink the Bismarck*. On 25 August 1959, while exercising off Ceylon with other navies, ***Hogue*** collided with the Indian light cruiser ***INS Mysore*** (ex-***HMS Nigeria***). Damage to ***Hogue*** was so severe that she was laid up and de-equipped at Singapore, before being sold on 7 March 1962 to Messrs Chaun Hup, Singapore for demolition.

Named in honour of the Battle of Lagos which took place in 1759 off the coast of Portugal, between the Royal Navy and a French fleet and resulted in a British victory, ***Lagos*** (YN: 1125) was laid down on 8 April 1943, launched 4 August 1944 and commissioned in November 1945. Too late for wartime service ***Lagos*** served in the Far East during 1946-47 before going into reserve at Devonport. She underwent modernisation and refit during 1954-56 prior to further service with the Home and Mediterranean Fleets from 1957-60. On 21 March 1960 she was added to the sales list and entered extended reserve at Portsmouth where she remained until approved for scrap in 1964. She was sold to McCellar of Glasgow in 1967.

The Colossus class aircraft carrier ***Venerable*** (YN: 1126) was laid down on 3 December 1942, launched on 30 December the following year and commissioned on 17 January 1945 before heading for service with the British Pacific Fleet's 11th Aircraft Carrier Squadron. She carried 48 aircraft in a single deck hangar. 16 of the class were ordered but only 8 were completed. At the end of the war ***Venerable*** transported Australian and Canadian prisoners of war back home. In 1948 she was sold to the Dutch Navy becoming ***Karel Doorman***. In 1968, after a boiler-room fire, which was repaired using spares from her incomplete sister ship ***Leviathan***, she was sold to the Argentine Navy and renamed ***ARA Veinticinco de Mayo***. She briefly served in the Falklands war until the sinking of the cruiser ***General Belgrano*** persuaded the Argentine Navy to stay in port. Thought to be out of service by 1990 she was scrapped in India around 1999.

Named after the Battle of Gravelines which took place in 1588, resulting in the English Navy defeating the Spanish Armada, ***Gravelines*** (YN: 1127) was laid down on 10 August 1943, launched in November 1944 and commissioned in June 1946. The Battle class were popular with their crews, being stabilised vessels, but there were complaints about lack of space, laundry facilities and having only one shower for 60 men. On completion of trials and defect rectification, ***Gravelines*** went directly into reserve where she remained until 1949. On 15 September 1949 she commissioned for service with the 3rd Destroyer Squadron serving with the Home and Mediterranean Fleets. In refit during 1953-54 she returned to reserve until 1958. A refit in 1958 was cancelled and she was scrapped at Rosyth in March 1961.

Taking her name from the Battle of Sluys which occurred in 1340 during the Hundred Years' War, and which resulted in a decisive English victory over the French fleet, ***Sluys*** (YN: 1128) was laid down on 24 November 1943, launched on 28 February 1944 and completed in September 1946. After service with the Home Fleet she was decommissioned in 1953 and remained in reserve until sold to Iran in 1967. Following a three year refit at Vosper Thornycroft of Southampton she became ***Artemiz***. Later, in 1985, she was renamed ***Damavand*** and, with a number of updates that included Russian-made missiles and radars, she remained in service until 1990.

Pictured in the River Mersey, heading out to Liverpool Bay around the date of her commissioning on 14 July 1944, ***Selene*** (YN: 1132), a Group III 'S' class submarine served largely in the Far East where she sank five ships. Post war she became a fast underwater target for training Royal Navy personnel in anti-submarine warfare. In this role her torpedo tubes were blanked over, armament removed and her conning tower reduced to a blister. She was sold for scrap in 1961. During WWII photography at Cammell Laird was restricted, which accounts for many wartime vessels being photographed in the Mersey.

The last 17 boats of the Group III 'S' class were significantly improved over the earlier boats. They had a stronger hull, carried more fuel and their armament was revised. ***HMS Solent*** (YN: 1134) was laid down on 7 May 1943, launched two days after D-Day on 8 June 1944 and entered service in September. In April 1945 she joined the 8th Submarine Flotilla in the Far East and was one of 35 Royal Navy submarines deployed in the Far East at that time, sinking around 15 ships. Post war she was streamlined to operate as a high speed target submarine. She was scrapped in 1961.

Commissioned towards the close of WWII on 14 June 1945, ***Saga*** (YN: 1141) had been laid down on 5 April 1944 and launched on 14 March 1945. She saw no wartime service and was sold to the Portuguese Navy in 1948, renamed ***NRP Náutilo*** and served until the late 1960s.

Cammell Laird were to build three 'A' class submarines. The 'A' class was intended to replace 'S' and 'T' class submarines with faster speed, deeper diving capability and improved endurance. ***HMS Affray*** (YN: 1143) was laid down on 16 January 1944, launched four months later but completed in November 1945, too late to see service in WWII. Currently she holds the distinction of being the last Royal Navy submarine to be lost at sea after going missing during a training exercise in the English Channel, in April 1951. It took two months to locate the submarine and her 75 men. Her normal crew was enlarged by a contingent of officer trainees. It was found that ***Affray*** was complete and undamaged externally apart from her snort tube, which was broken. The broken snort was recovered, tested and found to be defective, resulting in a conclusion that the failure occurred as the submarine was at periscope depth using the snort to intake air and exhaust fumes from her engines. The influx of an estimated 13 tons of water per minute would cause her loss. Today there is also speculation that the vessels poor condition at the time may have also been a factor in her loss.

Laid down in April 1944 ***Aeneas*** (YN: 1144) was launched on 25 October 1945 and completed on 31 July 1946. As with most of the class, ***Aeneas*** underwent modernisation in the late 1950s resulting in a fully streamlined hull with a bridge fin enclosing all masts, periscope standards and snort tube. All external torpedo tubes were removed and improved sonar and radar fitted. In modernised form she appeared in the 1967 Bond movie *You Only Live Twice* playing the submarine ***M1***. In 1972 she was used by Vickers for trials of the Submarine-Launched Airflight Missile (SLAM) system, an anti-aircraft system using a cluster of four Shorts Blowpipe missiles on an extendable mast fitted in a structure at the front of the conning tower. This allowed attacks against low-flying aircraft, primarily helicopters with dipping sonar, whilst the submarine was at periscope depth. The system was not developed further and the submarine was scrapped in 1974.

The third and final 'A' class submarine built by Cammell Laird, ***Alaric*** (YN: 1145), was laid down in May 1945, launched the following May and commissioned on 11 December 1946. Largely based in home waters for her entire service life she was modernised in the early 1960s before being sold for scrap to T. W. Ward in 1971. Originally 46 of the class were ordered but only 16 were completed. Cammell Laird were due to build a further five; ***Agate***, ***Aggressor***, ***Agile***, ***Aladdin*** and ***Alcestis*** but they were cancelled at the end of WWII. Her sistership ***Alliance*** has been preserved at the Submarine Museum, Gosport since 1981.

The first of the Type 12 anti-submarine frigates, ***Whitby*** (YN: 1229) was laid down in September 1952, launched on 2 July 1954 and commissioned in July 1956. The class of six were the first post war new construction frigates for the Royal Navy. They were designed as first rate ocean-going convoy escorts specialising in anti-submarine warfare and capable of tackling high speed submarine targets. ASW equipment comprised Type 174 search sonar; Type 162 target class sonar and Type 170 attack sonar. Two three-barrelled Mk10 Limbo ASW mortars were the main anti-submarine weapons. Initially they were also equipped with 12 x 21-inch torpedo tubes which were later removed. The high freeboard with raised forecastle gave the class a unique profile. Though soon outdated the hull would provide the basis for the follow-on Rothesay and Leander class. The cost of ***Whitby*** was £3.5 million. Initially she was built with a flat-fronted bridge. Her service included the first Cod War in March 1959. Between October 1962 and December 1963 she was based at Simonstown in South Africa and in the late 1960s served in the Far East. On 27 September 1973 during the second Cod War, she collided with the Icelandic patrol ***Thor***. She was paid off into reserve in December 1974 and was sold for scrap in 1979.

HMS Tenby (YN: 1233), a Whitby class, or Type 12 anti-submarine frigate, was laid down in 1953, launched on 4 October 1955 and commissioned on 15 December 1957. The kink aft of the forecastle allowed the heavy 4.5-inch Vickers Mk6 turret to be mounted lower in the ship. It also had the advantage of moving the bridge further back resulting in a more comfortable ride for the watchkeepers. Together with ***Salisbury*** in 1959 she became the first British warship to enter Lake Erie since the American War of Independence. In 1967 she appeared in the Bond movie *You Only Live Twice* where James Bond has a fake burial at sea. Set in Hong Kong, it was actually filmed in Gibraltar. In the early 1970s she was part of the Dartmouth Training Squadron. Paying off into reserve in 1972, a sale to Pakistan in 1975 fell through. She was scrapped in 1977 by T.W. Ward.

Cammell Laird built three Porpoise class submarines. This class of eight boats was the first designed and built for the Royal Navy after WWII and incorporated a number of features from the German Type XXI U-Boat. They were designed to counter Soviet submarines, were exceptionally quiet and could operate for prolonged periods. Armed with 8 x 21-inch torpedo tubes, 30 torpedoes could be carried. ***HMS Grampus*** (YN: 1238) was the first of these, being laid down in 1955 and launched in May 1957, commissioning in 1958. During March 1963 she spent 21 days under the Polar ice cap and became a harbour training ship between 1976 and 1979. She ended her days being sunk as a sonar target on 18 September 1980 in Loch Fyne where she remains to this day.

The only vessel in the Royal Navy to bear the name, ***Finwhale*** (YN: 1239) was laid down in September 1956, launched on 21 July 1959 and completed in August 1960. In the early 1960s she conducted two Polar ice patrols, once penetrating 95 miles under the ice. During service in the Far East she was fitted with an Oerlikon deck gun. Between 1979 and 1987 she was a harbour training ship, following which she was towed for scrap in Spain on 28 March 1988.

The final Porpoise class submarine built by Cammell Laird was ***Sealion*** (YN: 1265), laid down on 5 June 1958, launched on New Years Eve 1959 and completed in 1961. Clandestine operations, whether insertion of special forces or surveillance, were a speciality of these boats. Early in her career while conducting surveillance of Soviet fleet exercises in northern waters, ***Sealion*** was detected by Russian surface vessels, forced to the surface and escorted out of the exercise area. She was paid off in December 1987 and initially sold to the Education Trust "Inter Action" for deprived inner city youngsters, arriving at Chatham on 22 June 1988. This venture failed and she was sold for scrap in 1990.

A Type 12 frigate built for the Indian Navy, ***INS Talwar*** (YN: 1272) was laid down on 7 June 1957 and launched on 18 July 1958. She commissioned the following April. Her service included the Portuguese-Indian War and the Indo-Pakistani War of 1971. She was broken up in 1992. A second Type 12 was built for the Indian Navy by Harland & Wolff named ***INS Trishul***.

INS Talwar, shown here on launch day, 18 July 1958, with a slightly different launch ceremony than that usually seen in the UK. In India, ships have historically been launched with a Puja ceremony that dedicates the ship to a god and seeks blessings for her and her sailors. Historically, Hindu priests would perform the Puja ceremony at launch. In the 20th century a lady breaking a coconut on the bow of the vessel has taken over, as seen above.

The first of eight County class guided missile destroyers, ***Devonshire*** (YN: 1284) was laid down in March 1959 and launched by Princess Alexandra on 10 June 1960. It took a further two years to complete, commissioning on 15 November 1962. The class was based around the Seaslug long range guided missile system that, with magazines and handling areas, took up a vast amount of space internally. Development of Seaslug had started in 1949 and by the 1960s the missile was already dated. Twin Sea Cat systems provided close range air defence. The class was, however, regarded as one of the most attractive post war warships built for the Royal Navy. By the 1970s with large crews and dated systems the class began to be withdrawn. ***HMS Devonshire*** was the second to be paid off in 1978. A sale to Egypt never materialised and in July of 1984 she was sunk as a target by Tigerfish torpedoes from ***Splendid*** after being hit first by a Sea Eagle air-to-surface missile launched from a Sea Harrier.

HMS Ajax (YN: 1285) became one of the first of 26 Leander class frigates. Originally laid down as the Rothesay class frigate ***Fowey*** on 12 October 1959 ***Ajax*** was launched on 16 August 1962, and completed, to a revised design, in December 1963. A day after completing sea trials she successfully salvaged the Spanish freighter ***Llusanes*** that was in difficulties off the Casquets. After going to the Far East ***Ajax*** was in refit at Singapore from October 1965 to February 1966. She paid off in 1970 to be modernised at Devonport Dockyard during which time her gun turret was replaced by the Australian Ikara anti-submarine missile system. During the 1974 Turkish invasion of Cyprus, ***Ajax*** evacuated British citizens from Famagusta. Decommissioning in 1985 she remained a static training ship at Devonport until she was sold for scrap in 1988. Her anchor is on display in Ajax, Ontario, a town named after her WWII predecessor.

The Oberon class were a development of the earlier Porpoise class. Cammell Laird built four, starting with ***Odin***, (YN: 1288) which was laid down on 27 April 1959, launched on 4 November 1960 and commissioned in May 1962. Known for their quietness and fast underwater speed, some 27 Oberons were built, 13 for the Royal Navy, 6 for the Australian Navy, 3 each for Brazil and Canada and 2 for Chile. The last Oberons, operated by Canada and Australia, were decommissioned in 2000 with 8 of the class now preserved. ***HMS Odin*** left service in 1990 to be scrapped in Greece a year later.

HMS Odin, just after launch, being towed into Cammell Laird's wet basin where she would be fitted out. In the background right is Liverpool's Anglican Cathedral which would not be completed for another 18 years (total build time 80 years). The Oberon class submarines had a surfaced displacement of 2,000 tons, submerged displacement of 2,400 tons, a length of 295 feet and an armament of eight x 21-inch torpedo tubes (6 forward, 2 stern).

HMS Oracle (YN: 1297) was an Oberon class submarine laid down on 26 April 1960, launching on 26 September 1961 and completing February 1963. Improvements over the Porpoise class included glass fibre conning tower, higher grade steel in hull construction and better equipment fit. The class were intended for anti-submarine operations but also carried out many special forces missions. Decommissioned in 1993, ***HMS Oracle*** was scrapped at Pounds Yard, Portsmouth between 1997 and 2003.

HMS Opossum (YN: 1306) was laid down on 21 December 1961, launched in May 1963 and commissioned on 5 June 1964. She served in the 1991 Gulf War in Operation Granby. When she returned home she was flying the Jolly Roger indicating the fact that she had been involved in special forces operations. She also sported a sky blue/black camouflage scheme. On 14 July 1993 she collided with the fishing vessel ***Amber Rose*** off the coast of Scotland. A month later in August she visited the Russian port of Severomorsk, the first Royal Navy submarine to visit Russia since 1945. On 26 August 1993 ***Opossum*** decommissioned to be scrapped in 2001 at Pounds Yard, Portsmouth.

One of two combined boom defence and salvage vessels built by Cammell Laird for the Royal Maritime Auxilliary Service, ***RMAS Mandarin*** (YN: 1310) was built in 1964, the same time as her sister ***Pintail*** (YN: 1311). At 1,300 tons and with a speed of 10 knots they could lift 200 tons over their bows. ***RMAS Pintail*** was scrapped in 1994 and ***Mandarin*** left service in 1992.

By 1962 it was becoming apparent that Britain's airborne nuclear deterrent, in the form of the RAF's V-Bomber force, was unlikely to get through improving Russian air defences. The solution was to purchase the American Polaris submarine-launched missile system. The submarines would be the British Resolution class of four vessels which would be based on the Valiant class with an American-designed middle missile section. Vickers Armstrong, Barrow-in-Furness, would be the lead shipyard with Cammell Laird building two of the class. ***HMS Renown*** (YN: 1316) was laid down in June 1964, launched in February 1967 and commissioned in November 1968. Upgraded in 1982 during the Chevaline programme she was decommissioned and stored at Rosyth, being replaced by the Vanguard class Trident submarines.

The second Polaris submarine built by Cammell Laird was ***Revenge*** (YN: 1317) which was laid down on 19 May 1965, launched on 15 March 1968 and completed in December 1969. The build cost of ***Revenge*** was £38.6 million, just over £1 million pounds cheaper than ***Renown***. Upgraded to Chevaline in the late 1980s she was paid off in 1992, to be laid up at Rosyth. Each Polaris submarine had a crew of 143. The option of building a fifth member of the class, ***Royal Sovereign***, was cancelled in 1965. It would probably have been built at Cammell Laird and it is probable that the ordering of ***Conqueror*** from Cammell Laird not only kept up the tempo on the Polaris class but also compensated for the cancellation.

(Above left) ***HMS Revenge*** shows the different laying down procedures used for the Polaris boats on 19 May 1965. The class were built in sections, or blocks, in a similar manner to most modern ships. The image to the right shows the missile compartment with two tubes that will hold the Polaris missiles, of which 16 could be carried. This section of the submarine was basically of American design and inserted in between front and rear sections of what was basically a Valiant class hunter killer submarine. ***HMS Revenge*** had a surfaced displacement of 7,600 tons (8,500 submerged) with a length of 425 feet and was powered by one Rolls Royce PWR1 nuclear reactor.

Cammell Laird's ***Onyx*** (YN: 1319) was a replacement for a Chatham built Oberon boat of the same name that was transferred, whilst under construction, to Canada to become ***HMCS Ojibwa***. Laid down on 16 November 1964, she was launched on 18 August 1966 and commissioned in November 1967. During the 1982 Falklands War she was the only conventional submarine present, being used to land special forces. During one such operation she hit an underwater rock and although damage was minor a live torpedo was jammed in its tube until returning home to Portsmouth. The burnt out hulk of ***RFA Sir Galahad*** was sunk by ***Onyx***. Decommissioning in 1991 the submarine was initially preserved at Birkenhead by The Warship Preservation Trust. When they went into liquidation in 2006 the site was closed. She was moved to Barrow-in-Furness to form the centre-piece of a proposed submarine heritage centre. Unfortunately, this also failed and she was eventually scrapped, on the Clyde, in 2015.

The only British nuclear attack submarine not to be built at Barrow-in-Furness was ***Conqueror*** (YN: 1330). She was laid down at Cammell Laird on 5 December 1967, launched on 18 August 1969 and entered service in November 1971. She is famous for being the only nuclear submarine to sink a ship by torpedo during a conflict. During the Falklands War, on 2 May 1982, she sank the Argentine cruiser ***General Belgrano*** with the loss of 323 crew. Three WWII - designed Mk8 torpedoes were fired by ***Conqueror*** as her captain, Commander Chris Wreford-Brown, felt that the more modern Tigerfish torpedoes were too unreliable. In November 1985, ***Conqueror*** spent 18 days on a covert intelligence and ASW training war patrol, codenamed Operation 'Sheikh' covering the Barents Sea in which she carried out four simulated attacks on Soviet submarines with full fire control solutions. Post patrol analysis showed these attacks would have been successful. Decommissioning in 1990 she remains stored at Devonport awaiting a disposal solution. Her periscope and other equipment are on display at the Submarine Museum, Gosport.

The second of the 14 Type 42 guided missile destroyers, ***Birmingham*** (YN: 1358) was laid down on 28 March 1972 and launched on 30 July the following year. A Batch I Type 42, they replaced the eight County class destroyers and provided air defence for the fleet. Completed in December 1976, at a cost of some £31 million, she was equipped with the Sea Dart long range guided missile, a twin launcher being mounted behind the 4.5-inch gun. Though designed for the Westland Lynx helicopter the class initially carried the older Westland Wasp. ***HMS Birmingham*** was the first of the class to be decommissioned in 1999 and was sold for scrap in 2000.

Type 42 destroyer ***HMS Coventry*** (YN: 1359) was laid down in January 1973, launched on 21 June 1974 and completed on 10 November 1978. Part of the Falkland Islands Task Force in 1982, she was one of the first to head south and the first to enter the Total Exclusion Zone. In four weeks of conflict she shot down five fighter bombers, a helicopter and she sank a patrol boat. Her luck ran out on 25 May when deployed north-west of Falkland Sound. Together with the Type 22 frigate ***Broadsword*** they were acting as a Type 42/22 (Type 64!) combo with ***Coventry*** using her long range Type 965 radar to spot incoming Argentine air attacks, the Type 22 providing anti-missile/aircraft defence with her close range Sea Wolf missiles. Both vessels were stationed well ahead of the main task group hoping to draw attacks away from the aircraft carriers. The pair came under sustained Argentine air attack. During the second wave, ***Coventry*** turned to reduce her profile to the incoming aircraft, and in doing so inadvertently crossed ***Broadsword's*** track causing her Sea Wolf missiles to lose lock. ***HMS Coventry*** was hit by three bombs causing extensive damage. She sank in 30 minutes with the loss of 19 men with a further crewman dying a year later due to his injuries.

RFA Orangeleaf (YN: 1362) was the first of four commercial Stat32 single-hulled tankers that were taken over by the Ministry of Defence (MoD). Their role was that of support tanker with a single refuelling point each side. Launched in 1973 as ***MV Hudson Progress***, then renamed ***MV Balder London***, she was requisitioned for service in 1982 to take part in the Falklands conflict. In 1984 she was bare-boat chartered by the MoD and renamed ***RFA Orangeleaf*** being partly converted for RFA service at Falmouth. Full conversion took place on the Tyne between 1985 and 1986 when full RAS facilities and additional accommodation were added. She served in the 1991 Gulf war and in 2007 completed a Ship Life Extension Programme (SLEP) at Cammell Laird to extend her life until 2015. Arriving back at Cammell Laird on 9 June 2014 for a refit which was stopped two months later, the ship was then laid up until being withdrawn from the fleet on 30 September 2015. She was finally towed away, to be broken up at Turkey, by the tug ***Diavlos Pride,*** on 24 February 2016.

RFA Appleleaf (YN: 1363) was ordered by John Hudson Fuel and Shipping, laid down in November 1973 as ***Hudson Cavalier*** and launched on 24 July 1975. The company was having difficulties and could not afford to pay for the tankers they had ordered so, after sea trials, all the ships were laid up at Cammell Laird for sale. In 1978 the MoD expressed an interest in chartering two of the vessels for 10 years and, after military modifications, ***RFA Appleleaf*** was commissioned in June 1979. After her ten year lease ended the Royal Australian Navy chartered her for a further five years with an option to purchase. Becoming ***HMAS Westralia***, she commissioned in October 1989 and served in the 1991 Gulf War. A fire in 1998 killed four of the crew and in 2006 she was decommissioned and scrapped in Turkey during 2010.

Laid down as ***MV Hudson Deep*** in July 1974 and launched on 22 January 1976, ***RFA Brambleleaf*** (YN: 1364) was bare-boat chartered by the MoD on 20 February 1980. She was purchased outright in February 1983. Diverted from Armilla Patrol duties on 5 April 1982 to support Operation Corporate, the Falklands War, she initially joined Operation Paraquat, the retaking of South Georgia, on 25 April 1982. Later she served in Operation Telic in the second Gulf War in 2003. Destored at Portsmouth in 2007, she was laid up until August 2009 when she was towed to Ghent for recycling.

Ordered in 1973 and laid down in 1975 as the ***Hudson Sound***, the vessel was taken over by the MoD during construction, being launched on 27 October 1981 as ***RFA Bayleaf*** (YN: 1366). From commissioning in March 1982 she was on bare-boat charter and was soon involved in the Falklands war during which she replenished the Cunard liner ***QE2***. In 1986 she was part of the Global '86 Task Group deployment (TG 318.4) led by ***Illustrious***. She also participated in both Gulf wars and was purchased outright in 2001. Following the 2010 Strategic Defence Review she was paid off in April 2011. She was scrapped in Turkey during 2012 with apparently 98% of her structure re-cycled, the remaining 2% going to landfill.

HMS Liverpool (YN: 1374) was laid down in Cammell Laird's new construction hall on 5 July 1978, the same day the building was officially opened by Princess Anne. Launched on 25 September 1980 her commissioning was speeded up due to the Falkands War in 1982. She commissioned on 1 July, too late to see action, but she was still sent to the Falklands for 6 months. She saw service in the 2003 Iraq War and in 2011 spent seven months operating off Libya during which she became the first Royal Navy vessel to come under direct fire since the Falklands War, firing over 200 rounds from her main Vickers Mk8 gun. It was the final occasion that this type of gun was fired in anger by a Royal Navy warship. ***HMS Liverpool*** decommissioned in 2012 and was towed for scrap in Turkey in 2014.

HMS Liverpool's stern is seen emerging from the, then, new construction hall. The Type 42 destroyers were designed in the late 1960s to provide fleet area air defence using the Sea Dart missile system. The Sea Dart had a range of 46 miles (later upgraded to 92 miles) with a speed of Mach 2+ and went through three upgrades until 2012 when the system was withdrawn. It was replaced in service by the Sea Viper missile system fitted to Type 45 destroyers. ***HMS Liverpool*** was a Batch 2 Type 42 with a displacement of 4,820 tons, a length of 410 feet and powered by two Rolls-Royce Tyne gas turbines for cruising and two Rolls-Royce Olympus gas turbines when her top speed of 30 knots was required. Armament consisted of 1 x 4.5-inch gun, one twin Sea Dart missile system, 2 x 20mm guns, 2 x Vulcan Phalanx close range weapon system, 6 x torpedo tubes and a Lynx helicopter.

The only Batch III Type 42 built by Cammell Laird, ***HMS Edinburgh*** (YN: 1375) was laid down on 8 September 1980 and launched by Ann Heseltine, the wife of Michael Heseltine, in April 1983, before entering service in December 1985. She was one of four 'stretched' Type 42s which had an additional 16m of hull added forward of the bridge. This was from the experience gained in the Batch I and Batch II ships which were found to be poor seakeepers in heavy seas and only had space for 22 Sea Dart missiles. This change actually returned the class to how they had been intended when first designed, before defence cuts of the early 1970s. ***HMS Edinburgh*** took part in the second Gulf War in 2003 and was the last Type 42 in service, decommissioning in 2013 and leaving Portsmouth for scrapping in Turkey in 2015.

The last complete surface ship built for the Royal Navy at Cammell Laird was ***HMS Campbeltown*** (YN: 1378) which was laid down in December 1985, launched on 7 October 1987, commissioning on 27 May 1989. The Batch 3 Type 22 frigates were the largest frigates ever built for the Royal Navy, the design being modified in light of Falklands War experience. They were some 500 tons heavier than the Batch 2 and marked the return of the gun as main armament. She had a displacement of 5,300 tons and a length of 485 feet. In addition to the 4.5-inch gun, armament consisted of 2 sextuple Sea Wolf missile launchers, 8 x Harpoon missiles, 6 x torpedo tubes and up to two Lynx helicopters or a Sea King. During her service life the bell from the Second World War ***Campbeltown*** was loaned from Pennsylvania, USA, to the ship. The bell from the wartime Town class destroyer, made famous for her role in the St. Nazaire Raid, had been given to Campbeltown, Pennsylvania, as thanks for the vessel's loan as part of lend-lease. The 2010 Strategic Defence Review spelt the end for ***Campbeltown***, she was withdrawn in 2011 and towed for scrap in 2015.

In order to replace the Oberon class submarine it was decided to build 12 Upholder class submarines. These would be based on a Vickers design known as Type 2400, weighing 2,400 tons. Vickers had acquired Cammell Laird in 1985 and, as their Barrow-in-Furness yard was too busy building the Vanguard class submarines, many of the Upholder class would be built on the Mersey. ***HMS Unseen*** (YN: 1379) was laid down in August 1987, launched on 14 November 1989 and commissioned 20 July 1991. With the end of the Cold War it was decided that the Royal Navy would move forward with a pure nuclear powered submarine fleet, so in 1994 ***Unseen*** decommisioned to be sold to Canada in 1998, becoming ***HMCS Victoria***.

The plan for 12 Upholders was reduced to 10 and then, after the end of the Cold War, was further reduced to just four. ***HMS Ursula*** (YN: 1380) was laid down in January 1989, launched on 22 February 1991 and commissioned in May 1992. She served just over two years before decommissioning on 16 October 1994. Canada had been offered the entire class in 1993 but problems caused during re-activation, especially with welded pipes, delayed the handover until 1998. It was not until 2003, however, that ***Ursula*** recommissioned as ***HMCS Corner Brook***. A grounding incident put her out of service in 2011 and a three year repair commenced in 2014.

HMS Unicorn (YN: 1381) was laid down in February 1989. She became the last Royal Navy warship to be launched from Cammell Laird on 16 April 1992, commissioning on 25 June 1993. Just over a year later she decomissioned in October 1994, becoming ***HCMS Windsor*** in July 2001. With no further orders from the Ministry of Defence, and very little chance of any commercial shipbuilding work, Cammell Laird closed in 1993.

In 2010 Cammell Laird was one of six British shipyards contracted to produce blocks for the two Royal Navy Queen Elizabeth class aircraft carriers, the largest warships built for the Royal Navy and the largest since Cammell Laird's ***Ark Royal*** of 1955. The two ships were built in prefabricated blocks which would be assembled at Rosyth. Cammell Laird were contracted to build the flight deck blocks. Nine flight deck blocks were built for ***Queen Elizabeth*** and ten blocks for ***Prince of Wales***. In the photograph five blocks that were to form Centre Block 02 of the future ***Queen Elizabeth*** pass Liverpool's Three Graces on 28 May 2012. The combined weight of these blocks was 3,500 tons.

Two blocks for the future ***Prince of Wales*** await tow to Rosyth during October 2014 in Cammell Laird's wet basin. The two blocks, known as CB02 Ring F and Ring G, are 40m wide, 15m deep and 10m tall. Ring F weighs 942 tons whereas Ring G is 642 tons. The last blocks left Cammell Laird in 2015.

APPENDIX

NAVAL VESSELS BUILT BY CAMMELL LAIRD

Yard No	Name	Type	Completed
04	Euphrates	River Gunboat	1834 East India Co
05	Tigris	River Gunboat	1835 East India Co
18	Comet	River Gunboat	1839 East India Co
19	Meteor	River Gunboat	1839 East India Co
21	Nimrod	River Gunboat	1839 East India Co
22	Nitocris	River Gunboat	1839 East India Co
23	Assyria	River Gunboat	1839 East India Co
25	Ariadne	River Gunboat	1839 East India Co
26	Medusa	River Gunboat	1839 East India Co
27	Phlegethon	River Gunboat	1840 East India Co
28	Nemesis	River Gunboat	1840 East India Co
31	Dover	Mail Packet	1840
34	Soudan	Gunboat	1840
35	Albert	Gunboat	1840
36	Wilberforce	Gunboat	1840
42	Guadalupe	Frigate	1842 Mexico
46	Napier	River Gunboat	1843 East India Co
48	Conquer	River Gunboat	1844 East India Co
49	Meanee	River Gunboat	1844 East India Co
51	Birkenhead	Frigate	1846

Yard No	Name	Type	Completed
65	St Columba	Mail Packet	1847
69	Falkland	River Gunboat	1850 East India Co
70	Indus	River Gunboat	1850 East India Co
71	Jhelum	River Gunboat	1850 East India Co
72	Chenab	River Gunboat	1850 East India Co
115	Resolute	Troopship	1855
116	Assistance	Troopship	1855
129	Thais	Despatch Ship	1855
132	Syren	Despatch Ship	1855
143	Frere	River Gunboat	1856 East India Co
144	Havelock	River Gunboat	1856 East India Co
145	Outram	River Gunboat	1856 East India Co
146	Sir Henry Lawrence	River Gunboat	1856 East India Co
151	Beacon	Gunboat	1856
152	Brave	Gunboat	1856
153	Bullfinch	Gunboat	1856
154	Redbreast	Gunboat	1856
155	Rose	Gunboat	1856
156	Blazer	Gunboat	1856
157	Rainbow	Gunboat	1856

Yard No	Name	Type	Completed
158	Brazen	Gunboat	1856
159	Raven	Gunboat	1856
160	Rocket	Gunboat	1856
161	Cupid	Mortar Boat	1855
162	Blossom	Gunboat	1856
163	Gadfly	Gunboat	1856
164	Gnat	Gunboat	1856
165	Garland	Gunboat	1856
179-193	MF136-150	Mortar Boat	1856
243	Zambese	Gunboat	1859 Portugal
274	Chester	Tank Boat	1861
286	Orontes	Troopship	1862
290	Alabama	Sloop	1862 Confederate
291	Agincourt	Frigate-Iron Cased	1865
294	Scorpion	Frigate	1863
295	Wivern	Frigate	1863
296	Tien Tsin	Gunvessel	1863 China
297	Kwangtung	Gunvessel	1863 China
311	Zarco	Gunboat	1864 Portugal
321	Huascar	Monitor	1865 Peru
322	Unnamed	Launch	1865
325	Euphrates	Troopship	1866
326	Bahia	Turret Ship	1865 Brazil
327	Lima Barros	Turret Ship	1865 Brazil
330	Prins Hendrik	Frigate	1867 Netherlands

Yard No	Name	Type	Completed
346	Captain	Iron-Plated Turret Ship	1869
360	Stier	Ironclad Turret Ram	1868 Netherlands
361	Heiligerlee	Ironclad Turret Monitor	1868 Netherlands
362	Teazer	Gunboat	1868
364	Krokodil	Ironclad Turret Monitor	1868 Netherlands
366	Vanguard	Battleship-Ironclad	1869
403	Escort	Paddle-Tug	1873
404	Ant	Gunboat	1873
405	Cuckoo	Gunboat	1873
406	Hyaena	Gunboat	1873
407	Weazel	Gunboat	1873
408	Parana	Gunvessel	1873 Argentina
409	Uruguay	Gunvessel	1873 Argentina
412	El Plata	Ironclad Turret Ship	1874 Argentina
413	Los Andes	Ironclad Turret Ship	1874 Argentina
418	Libertad	Gunboat	1874 Argentina
419	Independencia	Gunboat	1874 Argentina
420	Malta	Paddle-Tug	1875
421`	Republica	Gunboat	1875 Argentina
422	Constitucion	Gunboat	1875
423	Rio Lima	Gunvessel	1875 Portugal
424	Tamega	Gunvessel	1875 Portugal
425	Sado	Gunvessel	1875 Portugal
426	Fu-sheng	Gunboat	1875 China
427	Chien-sheng	Gunboat	1875 China

Yard No	Name	Type	Completed
434	Griffon	Gunboat	1876
435	Falcon	Gunboat	1877
438	Sampson	Tug	1877
456	Mandovi	Gunvessel	1879 Portugal
457	Bengo	Gunvessel	1879 Portugal
471	Seahorse	Special Service Vessel	1880
477	Villarino	Transport	1879 Argentina
493	Clive	Troopship	1882
499	Supply	Tank Vessel	1881
506	Albacore	Sloop	1883
507	Mistletoe	Sloop	1883
508	Watchful	Sloop	1883
517	Aetna	Paddle-Tug	1883
518	Meteor	Tug	1883
527	Liberal	Gunboat	1884 Portugal
528	Zaire	Gunboat	1884 Portugal
531	Ireland	Paddle-Tug	1885
535	Lawrence	Paddle-Tug	1886
537	Rattlesnake	Torpedo Boat	1886
539	Cacongo	Gunvessel	1886 Portugal
540	Massabi	Gunvessel	1886 Portugal
572	Almirante Lynch	Torpedo Gunboat	1890 Chile
573	Almirante Condell	Torpedo Gunboat	1890 Chile
574	Espora	Torpedo Gunboat	1890 Argentina
575	Rosales	Torpedo Gunboat	1890 Argentina

Yard No	Name	Type	Completed
577	Libertad	Battleship	1890 Argentina
578	Indepedencia	Battleship	1891 Argentina
579	Royal Oak	Battleship	1892
585	Onyx	Torpedo Gunboat	1892
586	Reynard	Torpedo Gunboat	1892
591	TB97	Torpedo Boat	1893
592	Minto	Despatch Vessel	1893
593	Almirante Simpson	Torpedo Gunboat	1896 Chile
595	Patria	Light Cruiser	1893 Argentina
596	Ferret	Torpedo Destroyer	1893
597	Lynx	Destroyer	1894
598	Banshee	Destroyer	1894
599	Contest	Destroyer	1894
600	Dragon	Destroyer	1894
603	Mars	Battleship	1896
604	Salvador Correia	Despatch Vessel	1895 Potugal
606	Quail	Torpedo Destroyer	1895
607	Sparrowhawk	Destroyer	1895
608	Thrasher	Destroyer	1895
609	Virago	Destroyer	1895
616	Capitan Orella	Destroyer	1896 Chile
617	Munoz Gamero	Destroyer	1896 Chile
618	Teniente Serrano	Destroyer	1896 Chile
619	Riquelme	Destroyer	1896 Chile
621	Earnest	Destroyer	1896

Yard No	Name	Type	Completed
622	Griffon	Destroyer	1896
623	Locust	Destroyer	1895
624	Panther	Destroyer	1897
625	Seal	Destroyer	1897
626	Wolf	Destroyer	1897
627	Fulton	Minelayer	1897 Argentina
629	Express	Destroyer	1897
630	Glory	Battleship	1899
633	Orwell	Destroyer	1898
635	Mutine	Sloop	1899
636	Rinaldo	Sloop	1899
637	Som	Torpedo Destroyer	1899 Russia
638	Exmouth	Battleship	1901
639	Lively	Destroyer	1900
640	Sprightly	Destroyer	1900
644	Merino Jarpa	Destroyer	1901 Chile
645	Capitan O'Brien	Destroyer	1901 Chile
649	Foyle	Destroyer	1903
650	Itchen	Destroyer	1903
651	Arun	Destroyer	1903
652	Blackwater	Destroyer	1903
653	Topaze	Cruiser	1903
654	Diamond	Cruiser	1904
655	Pathfinder	Scout Vessel	1904
658	Patrol	Scout Vessel	1904

Yard No	Name	Type	Completed
659	Liffey	Destroyer	1904
660	Moy	Destroyer	1904
661	Ouse	Destroyer	1905
663	Test	Destroyer	1905
664	Stour	Destroyer	1905
667	Cossack	Destroyer	1907
671	Swift	Destroyer	1907
691	Renard	Destroyer	1909
692	Wolverine	Destroyer	1909
693	Racoon	Destroyer	1910
698	Aetos	Destroyer	1912 Greece
699	Leon	Destroyer	1912 Greece
700	Panthir	Destroyer	1912 Greece
701	Lerax	Destroyer	1912 Greece
713	Lapwing	Destroyer	1911
714	Lizard	Destroyer	1911
720	Adamant	Tender	1911
721	Alecto	Tender	1911
728	Five Horse Boats		1908
770	Floating Dock		1912
772	Melbourne	Cruiser	1912
775	Audacious	Battleship	1912
786	Garland	Destroyer (hull only)	1913
803	Caroline	Light Cruiser	1914
809	Birkenhead	Cruiser	1915

Yard No	Name	Type	Completed
810	Kempenfelt	Destroyer	1915
811	Chester	Cruiser	1916
812	Castor	Light Cruiser	1915
813	Constance	Light Cruiser	1915
814	E41	Submarine	1915
815	E42	Submarine	1915
816	E45	Submarine	1916
817	E46	Submarine	1916
818	Gabriel	Torpedo Boat Destroyer	1915
819	Ithuriel	Torpedo Boat Destroyer	1915
820	Abdiel	Torpedo Boat Destroyer	1915
822	Parker	Torpedo Boat Destroyer	1916
823	Grenville	Torpedo Boat Destroyer	1916
824	Hoste	Torpedo Boat Destroyer	1916
825	Seymour	Torpedo Boat Destroyer	1916
826	Saurnarez	Torpedo Boat Destroyer	1916
828	Caledon	Light Cruiser	1917
829	Valentine	Torpedo Boat Destroyer	1917
830	Valhalla	Torpedo Boat Destroyer	1917
831	Scott	Torpedo Boat Destroyer	1917
832	L7	Submarine	1917
833	L8	Submarine	1917
837	Bruce	Flotilla Leader	1918
838	Douglas	Flotilla Leader	1918
849	Campbell	Flotilla Leader	1918

Yard No	Name	Type	Completed
850	Mackay	Flotilla Leader	1918
851	Malcolm	Flotilla Leader	1919
870	Cairo	Light Cruiser	1918
871	Capetown	Light Cruiser	1919
872	H33	Submarine	1918
873	H34	Submarine	1918
876	R11	Submarine	1918
877	R12	Submarine	1918
904	Rodney	Battleship	1925
941	Phoenix	Submarine	1929
983	Achilles	Cruiser	1932
989	Sealion	Submarine	1934
990	Salmon	Submarine	1934
992	Fearless	Destroyer	1934
993	Foresight	Destroyer	1934
1008	Hardy	Flotilla Leader	1936
1011	Spearfish	Submarine	1936
1012	Ark Royal	Aircraft Carrier	1937
1015	Inglefield	Flotilla Leader	1936
1021	Misiones	Destroyer	1938 Argentina
1022	Santa Cruz	Destroyer	1938 Argentina
1025	Aldersdale	Tanker	1937
1026	Prince of Wales	Battleship	1939
1027	Thetis	Submarine	1938
1028	Trident	Submarine	1938

Yard No	Name	Type	Completed
1033	Dido	Cruiser	1939
1036	Taku	Submarine	1939
1038	Gurkha	Destroyer	1940
1039	Lively	Destroyer	1941
1040	Talisman	Submarine	1940
1041	Charybdis	Cruiser	1941
1043	Atherstone	Escort Vessel	1939
1044	Berkeley	Escort Vessel	1940
1047	Argonaut	Cruiser	1941
1048	Blencathra	Escort Vessel	1940
1049	Brocklesby	Escort Vessel	1940
1050	Thrasher	Submarine	1940
1051	Thorn	Submarine	1941
1052	Tempest	Submarine	1941
1053	Empire	Steel Tanker	1940
1054	Dewdale	Tanker	1941
1055	Badsworth	Escort Vessel	1941
1056	Beaufort	Escort Vessel	1941
1057	Safari	Submarine	1941
1058	Sahib	Submarine	1942
1059	Saracen	Submarine	1942
1062	Sybil	Submarine	1942
1063	Seadog	Submarine	1942
1064	Raider	Destroyer	1942
1065	Rapid	Destroyer	1942

Yard No	Name	Type	Completed
1069	MLC79	Motor Landing Craft	1940
1070	MLC80	Motor Landing Craft	1940
1071	MLC81	Motor Landing Craft	1940
1072	MLC82	Motor Landing Craft	1941
1073	MLC83	Motor Landing Craft	1941
1074	MLC84	Motor Landing Craft	1941
1075	MLC85	Motor Landing Craft	1941
1076	MLC86	Motor Landing Craft	1941
1077	Aldenharn	Escort Vessel	1941
1078	Belvoir	Escort Vessel	1941
1079	TLC5	Tank Landing Craft	1940
1080	TLC6	Tank Landing Craft	1940
1081	Glaisdale	Escort Vessel	1942
1082	Eskdale	Escort Vessel	1942
1083	Sea Nymph	Submarine (P223)	1942
1084	Sickle	Submarine (P224)	1942
1085	Simoon	Submarine (P225)	1942
1086	MLC131	Motor Landing Craft	1941
1087	MLC132	Motor Landing Craft	1941
1088	MLC133	Motor Landing Craft	1941
1089	MLC134	Motor Landing Craft	1941
1090	TLC23	Tank Landing Craft	1941
1091	TLC24	Tank Landing Craft	1941
1092	TLC111	Tank Landing Craft	1941
1093	TLCI112	Tank Landing Craft	1941

Yard No	Name	Type	Completed
1094	Scorpion	Destroyer	1942
1095	Scourge	Destroyer	1942
1096	Stubborn	Submarine (P238)	1942
1097	Surf	Submarine (P239)	1942
1098	Syrtis	Submarine (P241)	1943
1099	Teazer	Destroyer	1943
1100	Tenacious	Destroyer	1943
1101	Cygnet	Sloop	1942
1102	Kite	Sloop	1942
1103	Ulysses	Destroyer	1943
1104	Undaunted	Destroyer	1943
1106	Empire MacColl	Merchant Aircraft Carrier	1943
1107	Stoic	Submarine (P231)	1943
1108	Stonehenge	Submarine (P232)	1943
1109	Storm	Submarine (P233)	1943
1110	Stratagem	Submarine (P234)	1943
1111	Salveda	Salvage Vessel	1943
1114	Spirit	Submarine (P245)	1943
1115	Statesman	Submarine (P246)	1943
1117	Zambesi	Destroyer	1943
1118	Zealous	Destroyer	1944
1119	Ark Royal	Aircraft Carrier	1955
1122	Sturdy	Submarine (P248)	1945
1123	Stygian	Submarine (P249)	1945
1124	Hogue	Destroyer	1944
1125	Lagos	Destroyer	1944
1126	Venerable	Aircraft Carrier	1943
1127	Gravelines	Destroyer	1944
1128	Sluys	Destroyer	1945
1129	Subtle	Submarine (P251)	1944
1130	Supreme	Submarine (P252)	1944
1131	Seascout	Submarine (P253)	1944
1132	Selene	Submarine (P254)	1944
1134	Solent	Submarine (P262)	1944
1135	Sleuth	Submarine (P261)	1944
1136	Sidon	Submarine (P259)	1944
1137	Spearhead	Submarine (P263)	1944
1138	Spur	Submarine (P265)	1945
1139	Scorcher	Submarine (P258)	1944
1140	Sanguine	Submarine (P266)	1945
1141	Saga	Submarine (P257)	1945
1142	Springer	Submarine (P264)	1945
1143	Affray	Submarine	1945
1144	Aeneas	Submarine	1945
1145	Alacric	Submarine	1944
1161	LCT7043	Landing Craft	1944
1162	LCT7044	Landing Craft	1944
1163	LCT7045	Landing Craft	1944
1164	LCT7046	Landing Craft	1944
1165	LCT7047	Landing Craft	1944

Yard No	Name	Type	Completed
1166	LCT7048	Landing Craft	1944
1167	LCT7049	Landing Craft	1944
1168	LCT7050	Landing Craft	1944
1229	Whitby	Frigate	1954
1233	Tenby	Frigate	1955
1238	Grampus	Submarine	1957
1239	Finwhale	Submarine	1959
1265	Sealion	Submarine	1959
1272	Talwar	Frigate	1959 India
1284	Devonshire	Destroyer	1962
1285	Ajax	Frigate	1962
1288	Odin	Submarine	1962
1297	Oracle	Submarine	1962
1306	Opossum	Submarine	1963
1310	Mandarin	Salvage Vessel	1963
1311	Pintail	Salvage Vessel	1963

Yard No	Name	Type	Completed
1316	Renown	Polaris Submarine	1969
1317	Revenge	Polaris Submarine	1969
1319	Onyx	Submarine	1967
1330	Conqueror	Nuclear Submarine	1971
1358	Birmingham	Destroyer	1976
1359	Coventry	Destroyer	1978
1362	Orangeleaf	Auxiliary	1975
1363	Appleleaf	Auxiliary	1979
1365	Brambleleaf	Auxiliary	1980
1366	Bayleaf	Auxiliary	1982
1374	Liverpool	Destroyer	1982
1375	Edinburgh	Destroyer	1985
1378	Campbeltown	Frigate	1989
1379	Unseen	Submarine	1991
1380	Ursula	Submarine	1992
1381	Unicorn	Submarine	1993

Index